The **COUNTRY LIVING** Needlework Collection

sewing

The **COUNTRY LIVING** Needlework Collection

sewing

projects • techniques • motifs

Sue Thompson

Quadrille

page 1: Garden Pavilion (see page 42)
page 2: Billowing Curtain (see page 32)

Illustrations · Lucy Su
Technical drawings · Stephen Dew
Detail photography · Peter Cassidy, Dave King

First published in 1995 by
Quadrille Publishing Limited
Alhambra House,
27-31 Charing Cross Road,
London WC2H 0LS

This paperback edition first published in 1999

Published in association with the National Magazine Company Limited
Country Living is a trademark of the National Magazine Company Limited

Publishing Director · Anne Furniss
Art Director · Mary Evans
Managing Editor · Jane O'Shea
Editor · Clare Carter
Copy Editor · Sarah Widdicombe
Art Editor · Christine Wood
Production Assistant · Kate Walford

British Library Cataloguing-in-Publication Data
A catalogue record for this book is available
from the British Library.

ISBN 1 899988 64 5

Printed in Spain

contents

Introduction

Years ago, most women started to learn to sew as young children, so that by the age of 10 or 11 they were already able to make simple clothes and household articles. They also possessed the confidence to move on to more complex sewing, secure in the knowledge that help and advice would be readily available from friends and relations. Life has changed, however, and these traditional sewing skills are rapidly disappearing, so that today comparatively few people can cope with more than stitching on a button or mending a hem. Schools also seem to have abandoned teaching practical sewing skills, while evening classes in sewing are becoming a rarity, to the point where now the first hurdle in learning to sew is to find a teacher with the necessary skills.

This book is designed to fill the gap. It is written for the beginner and assumes virtually no previous knowledge of sewing. It starts at the beginning and works through all the different aspects of sewing needed to make simple household items, using straightforward, step-by-step instructions for everything you will need to know, complemented by clearly illustrated examples.

Choosing fabrics and equipment, using pattern diagrams, cutting out fabric, sewing and finishing seams, dealing with corners and curves, and making facings are just some of the essential topics covered in the first two chapters. The following chapter is devoted to the many different types of fastening which can be used, and includes full instructions for two distinct types of decorative button which you can make yourself. The final chapter then covers some of the easier trimmings and decorative techniques which can be used to add the finishing touches to your creations.

Each chapter includes projects incorporating the various techniques. These range from the small and simple, such as the Cloth and Napkins on page 36, to others which appear quite large and impressive, like the Garden Pavilion on pages 42–45, but do not be daunted – the comprehensive instructions make them all easy to put together.

In fact, by the time you have worked through this book, and made up some of the designs, you will no longer be a beginner, but a fully fledged home sewer.

Getting started

Choosing the right fabric for a project is crucial to success, so one of the first things you will need to do is to learn to discriminate between the many types available. The easiest way to do this is to handle as many as possible, look around you now: there are probably five or six fabrics close by, but you may never have consciously felt them – it is likely that they will all feel quite different from each other. If you wonder why, read on: this chapter explains how fabrics are made, describes the materials from which they are made and gives advice on how to select the right one for your design.

Finding the right fabric is just the start; although home sewing doesn't need masses of specialist equipment, there are a few necessities that you may need to buy or borrow before starting a sewing project. And, finally, we've included a guide to patterns and a selection of the basic stitches, both hand and machine which you may wish to use.

types of fabric

The shops are full of so many wonderful fabrics that it is very exciting, if a little daunting, trying to choose the right one for a particular purpose. Of course, you will be able to reject many straight away as unsuitable in colour or design, but there will still be a vast array from which to choose. To help you make a successful selection, you will need to know something about the two main factors determining the basic characteristics of any fabric. These are, firstly, the type and weight of fibre used, and secondly, the way this fibre is turned into cloth.

Fibres

The basic material from which all textiles are made is fibre. This is spun into yarn which is then used to weave or knit the fabric. Fibres used for making textiles come from three main sources: animal, vegetable (plant) and man-made.

Animal fibres

Wool is the most widely used animal fibre, producing fabrics ranging from the finest nun's veiling to hairy tweeds. Silk is used for a huge variety of fabrics including satin, taffeta, chiffon, velvet and brocades. Cashmere and Angora goat's wool are used for clothing.

Vegetable (plant) fibres

Cotton is probably the most widely used vegetable fibre. Liberty lawn is an example of a fine cotton fabric; at the other end of the scale are the thick, slub cottons widely used for curtains and loose covers. Velvet, chintz, cambric and muslin are all fabrics which can be made from cotton fibre.

Linen is made from the flax plant. It feels flat and cool to the touch, improves with washing and is extremely hardwearing, making it ideal for furnishings. Linen crumples easily and so is often mixed with other fibres, such as polyester, to counteract this. Other plant fibres such as hemp, jute and ramie are increasingly popular.

Man-made fibres

Man-made fibres divide neatly into two categories. The first is made from a range of artificial materials and used to produce fabrics such as polyester, nylon and terylene. These are usually very hardwearing, wash easily and require no ironing, but they tend not to hang well and are difficult to press satisfactorily. These man-made fabrics are used to replace a wide variety of fabrics traditionally made from cotton, wool or linen, although they rarely achieve the quality associated with the originals.

The second category of man-made fibres is produced from woodpulp; the resulting fabric is called rayon or viscose. Unlike other man-made fabrics, it is very comfortable to wear but not hard-wearing enough for use on furnishings.

Weaves

Fabrics fall into two main categories: knitted and woven. Knitted fabrics are more commonly used for dressmaking than home furnishing. They must be stitched with a zigzag stitch so that the seams stretch with the fabric.

The way in which a fabric is woven and how the yarn or filament is spun usually affects the character of the final result more than the fibre from which it is made. A plain cross weave fabric has warp threads along the length of the fabric and weft threads woven across them. Twill fabrics appear to have a diagonal weave, caused by weaving the weft thread over an uneven number of warp threads.

It is important to differentiate between weave and fibre. Satin, for instance, is the name of a weave, and is more likely now to be made from man-made fibres or cotton ('sateen') than from silk, but whatever fibre is used the weave will be the same, showing the natural sheen of the yarn to best advantage. Similarly, velvet is as likely to be made from rayon or other man-made fibres as from silk or cotton.

choosing fabrics

The most important thing to bear in mind when choosing and using fabrics is that there are no fixed rules, and your choice will depend largely on your own visual ideas, combined with the fashion influences of the day. You will also need to think about the practical demands of the project you have in mind, bringing your knowledge of fabric types and characteristics into play. Finally, you will need to consider the effects of colour and pattern on the design you are creating.

Getting the feel

One of the best ways of discovering which fabrics are suitable for particular purposes is to look at and handle as many fabrics as possible.

Look at the fabrics around you: bedcovers, curtains, tablecloths. Feel the surface texture and how this varies from one fabric to another: is it smooth or rough, matt or glossy? Is the fabric thick or thin, does it hang heavily or lightly? Do you prefer curtains which hang in lots of folds or very few? How do the frills look on a loose cover or cushion? A thinner fabric will often require more fullness than a thicker one to give an equally generous effect. Try to get used to relating the weight of different fabrics to how they hang. Don't be afraid to test the fabric qualities: if it's for a cushion, crush it in your hand, if it's for curtains, see how a length drapes.

Buying fabrics   In order to avoid costly mistakes when shopping for fabrics, you will need to follow some sort of procedure and carry out certain checks. Make sure you take with you:

- Your ideas on the type of fabric you require, based on both aesthetic and practical considerations.
- Swatches for colour matching. It is impossible to carry colours in your head.
- Tape measure.
- Diagram showing the pattern layout, with measurements and the total amount of fabric needed.

Once you have made a preliminary choice of fabric, remember:

- If you have chosen a fabric with a very large pattern (either printed or woven), allow extra fabric for matching the repeats (see page 20).

- If the fabric has a one-way design, all the pattern pieces must be laid the same way up and you will have to allow extra fabric to account for this. If you are a beginner, these fabrics are probably best avoided at first.
- If you will be cutting lots of small pieces, avoid large prints, as the design may end up looking very muddled.

Finally, if you do fall in love with a particular fabric and it is wildly unsuitable, do not give up all hope – it is sometimes possible to adapt the fabric or your design in some way to make its use feasible.

colour &
pattern

Because most people do not choose colours and patterns very frequently, they can find it a daunting prospect, and often have no strategy for approaching the task. Look into any designer's studio, however, and you will find a mass of fabric swatches, trimming samples and colour cards for reference, piles of magazines, catalogues or books on many subjects for inspiration and pinboards covered with all sorts of bits and pieces which have caught the designer's eye. Of course, you cannot become a designer overnight simply by collecting these things, but it is a good point from which to start.

Colour

We normally see colours in groups, and adjacent colours affect each other. A warm colour surrounded by cool ones usually appears even hotter; it may make the cool ones appear drab, or it may create an accent. Accent colours might be pale, or dark, or vivid, but they invariably contrast sharply with the rest of the group.

The cold effect of a thin, sharp blue, for example, can be neutralized by combining it with richer and warmer colours. Alternatively, walls of the same icy blue may be used to create a cooling effect in a hot, sunny room, although touches of warmer and brighter colours might be needed to avoid a flat, lifeless colour scheme.

Pattern

Different patterns have different effects on us. Large patterns with lots of movement and contrasting colours create a lively effect, but may be irritating if overdone. At the other extreme, rooms done out in diminutive patterns and soft colours are often boring rather than peaceful, although they can usually be brought to life by adding a contrasting colour or pattern.

Because they can be exhilarating if seen for just a few minutes, and the contrast in scale is exciting, huge patterns can be used to good effect in 'passing through' rooms like halls. It can also be fun to cover items such as small chairs with large patterns.

An easy way to make widely differing patterns mix successfully is to choose groups with a similar theme. For example, combine multi-coloured florals, checks, stripes and dots, all with a black background, or select a variety of patterned and plain fabrics with the same or a similar colour scheme.

Inspiration

Keep an eye open for inspiration wherever you go. Notice the way in which colour and pattern have been used, and be critical – why does one mixture work, and another fail?

Make notes on your pinboard, with fabric swatches and trimmings to remind you of successful groups of colours and patterns. Experiment with the relative proportions of each colour, and with mixtures of different patterns and contrasting textures. If a scheme isn't working, try adding a bold contrasting colour, perhaps with piping or another trimming.

choosing equipment

Listed below is the equipment you will need to begin sewing. It goes without saying that you will achieve the best results using good-quality equipment, which will also last longer, so do not be tempted to economize at this stage by purchasing bargains from market stalls. Even if you have never done any sewing you will probably already have some of the items, such as paper-cutting scissors and a steam iron, so it is unlikely that you will have to go out and buy everything on the list.

In addition, you will need a large, smooth table on which to draw out patterns and cut out fabric. Avoid polished surfaces: it is difficult to work on a table covered with a protective cloth, but without this the surface could easily become scratched. You will also need somewhere to store all your equipment. This should be dry, to prevent scissors and other metal items rusting, and dark, as sunlight will eventually cause threads to rot.

Measuring and marking out

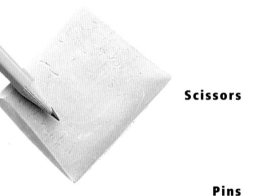

You will need:
- Dressmaker's tape measure.
- Long ruler or metre rule (yardstick), for drawing straight lines on patterns.
- Set square (optional).
- Pencils and tailor's chalk.

- Large sheets of paper, on which to draw out patterns. Lightweight squared paper made specially for the purpose is ideal, as the grid provides useful guidelines, but newsprint (widely available from art shops) will do.

Scissors

Ideally, you should have three pairs:
- Dressmaker's shears, for cutting out fabric. Do not use them for paper.
- Long bladed scissors, for cutting paper. Kitchen scissors are fine.

- Tiny, sharply pointed sewing scissors, for cutting threads, unpicking seams, or trimming corners and seams.

All these scissors should be very sharp and comfortable to use in the hand.

Pins

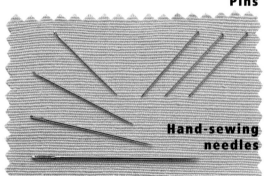

Buy long, thin, sharply pointed pins, as these are a pleasure to use – this is hard to appreciate until you have tried to use short, thick ones, which feel like pushing pokers into the fabric! Pins with coloured glass heads look pretty and are useful if you cannot see very well; otherwise, they are a nuisance because they do not lie flat against the fabric, so cause a pinned seam to become puckered.

Do keep pins in their own tin, as it is irritating to keep picking up needles by mistake. Make sure the tin is damp-proof, to prevent the pins rusting.

Hand-sewing needles

Keep a selection of hand-sewing needles of various sizes and with different-shaped eyes to accommodate different weights of thread. Packets of mixed needles are a good buy if you do not already have any. Keep needles in a damp-proof box or tin, to prevent them from rusting, or use a felt needlecase.

Sewing machine

If you do not already have a sewing machine, it is a good idea to borrow one first to get the feel of using it before choosing one for yourself. A machine that will do straight, zigzag and reverse stitches is all that is needed, although an automatic buttonhole facility is very useful. Machines that make all sorts of fancy stitches are not necessary. If, on the other hand, your machine only does straight stitch, you will still be able to make all the projects in this book by doing some extra hand finishing.

When buying a sewing machine, go to a specialist shop where you will be able to choose between several different makes and models. Try out the ones you like on several different thicknesses and types of fabric to test if they will stitch equally well on all of them, before making your final choice.

Do remember to oil your machine frequently and to clean out the bobbin case with a lint brush (following the manufacturer's instructions).

Machine needles

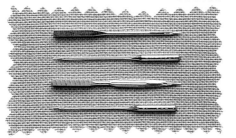

These come in a range of sizes: use fine needles for fine fabrics and thicker needles for thicker fabrics. Finer needles have smaller eyes so will only take fine threads, while thicker needles have larger eyes and will take thicker threads. The thread must run freely through the needle; if it does not, use either a finer thread or a thicker needle.

Keep a supply of machine needles of various sizes in stock. Beware: there are several sizing systems for machine needles, so make sure you buy the right ones for your machine. Before starting a new project, check that the needle you are using is sharp and change it if it is not: a blunt or snagged needle will not make good stitches.

Thread

Threads should look smooth and have a slight sheen. To work out which threads to use with which fabrics, compare several reels: use the finer threads with lighter fabrics and the thicker threads with heavier fabrics.

Haberdashery shops usually stock only one brand of polyester machine thread in just two weights – the finer one will do for all but the heaviest fabrics as, although fine, it is very strong. Avoid using too heavy a thread, as this makes the seams bulky and tends to stiffen them. If, however, you plan to make something which is going to take a lot of hard wear, or are using a very heavy fabric, it is worth using an extra-strong thread. Use the same thread for hand finishing as for machining.

- Buttonhole thread is extra thick, well twisted and much harder wearing than ordinary thread, and it is surprising how much better buttonholes look when made with it, especially on heavy fabrics. Unfortunately, it is too thick for making buttonholes on finer fabrics, so here use the same thread as for making up.

- It is not necessary to use silk thread for silk fabric except for decoration.
- Do not be tempted to buy cheap thread, especially if it is unbranded. This is often overlocking thread, or old and rotten, and in either case is too weak for machining. Use it only for tacking seams together by hand or machine.

Iron and ironing board

A steam iron is one of the great modern inventions. Choose one which produces plenty of steam, as this really helps to make professional-looking, flat seams and sharp edges. Do ensure that the bottom of the iron is clean so that it can glide smoothly. A well-padded board turns ironing into a pleasure whereas ironing on an unpadded board is a miserable experience. Remove the ironing board cover and use several layers of old blanket or towel to pad the surface, ensure the layers are smooth and stretch the ironing board cover tightly over the padding. Tie the cover drawstring or tapes securely under the board.

pattern diagrams

Full instructions for laying out a pattern and cutting out the fabric accurately are given on pages 20–21. These apply equally whether you are using scaled-up pattern pieces or commercial paper patterns, which are supplied full size, and it is important to follow them carefully to achieve the best results. Commercial patterns usually include a variety of layouts for different fabric widths. It is worth opening and reading the pattern instructions before buying an unusual width of fabric.

Diagram details

The pattern diagrams on pages 98–108 each show the pattern pieces needed for a particular project, drawn to a reduced scale, as shown in the sample diagram (fig 1). They are marked out in squares to make it easier to enlarge, or 'scale up', the pattern pieces to full size before they are used for cutting out the fabric. The diagrams show:

- The scale to use, marked on a square, here one square equals 5cm (2in);
- The reduced pattern pieces (to be scaled up to full size);
- The position for each pattern piece on the fabric. Lay the 'straight grain' line parallel to the selvedge.

Each diagram is fully annotated to provide all the information needed to scale up the pattern. Any special cutting-out instructions needed for the project are also given. Seam allowances of 1.5cm (⅝in) are included on all the patterns unless otherwise specified.

The exact amount of fabric required of a specified width is also shown with the relevant pattern. The only exception is where a project is made to fit an existing item of your own, such as the Picnic Basket Lining on page 36. In these instances, the instructions explain how you can work out the quantity of fabric you will require by taking your own specific set of measurements.

fig 1

120cm (48in) wide fabric

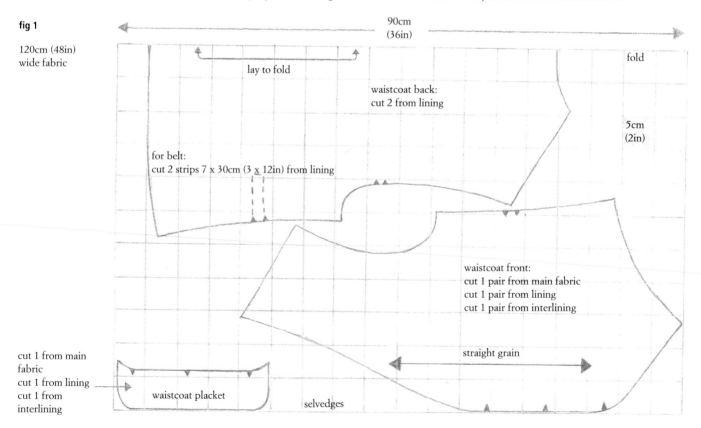

90cm (36in)

lay to fold

waistcoat back:
cut 2 from lining

fold

5cm (2in)

for belt:
cut 2 strips 7 x 30cm (3 x 12in) from lining

waistcoat front:
cut 1 pair from main fabric
cut 1 pair from lining
cut 1 pair from interlining

straight grain

cut 1 from main fabric
cut 1 from lining
cut 1 from interlining

waistcoat placket

selvedges

Scaling up

Mark out a large sheet of paper, such as newsprint, in squares of the size indicated on the pattern diagram. Alternatively, use dressmaker's lightweight squared paper with grids printed in metric or imperial squares.

Choose a pattern piece from the diagram which has at least one straight edge. Measure this edge and mark it on a line close to the edge of the paper, using the squares as a guide. Measure off an adjacent line on the pattern piece and draw it out on the paper. Continue in this way until you have completed the pattern piece, so that whatever appears in each small square is reproduced, 'scaled up', in the corresponding larger square (fig 2).

For pattern pieces with no straight edges or with mainly curved lines, start near one side of the paper and make marks on the grid lines corresponding to those on the diagram. Then make marks between the grid lines to enable you to draw in the curves accurately. Continue in this way, gradually extending all the curves until the pattern piece is completely drawn in (fig 3).

Transfer all line and markings from one small square to corresponding large square.

fig 2

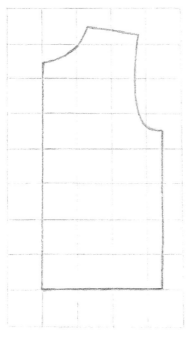

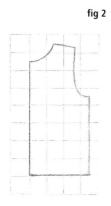

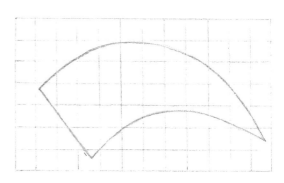

fig 3

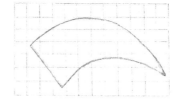

Annotating the pattern

• Grain lines are marked on the pattern diagram to show you the direction in which the 'grain' or 'thread' of the fabric should run. Mark these on to the scaled-up pattern pieces.
• By matching one to another, notches show how the cut-out pattern pieces fit together. Mark them accurately on to the scaled-up pattern pieces.
• When 'lay to fold' is written on one side of a pattern piece on the diagram, it means that the piece must be laid with that edge directly against a fold in the fabric, and will therefore be cut to double the size of the pattern piece. Write this on the scaled-up pattern piece (see fig 1 on page 20).
• Finally, mark each pattern piece with the name of both the project and the piece, as shown on the diagram. It is also helpful to add some identification, such as the date and a description of the fabric, in case you want to use the pattern again at a later date.

19

marking & cutting out

It is important to mark and cut out the fabric accurately or the pieces may not fit together properly. For some curious reason, home sewers who are otherwise neat and thorough are often very careless about cutting out, and the result is far from accurate. So, take plenty of time, and lay out all the pattern pieces before cutting to check that they do fit on to the material. Use sharp dressmaker's shears, follow the steps below carefully and cut clean, smooth edges on all the pieces.

Notches are sometimes regarded as a problem, but they are actually very easy to deal with if every notch is marked and clipped as described opposite. Do not be tempted to cut notches as little triangles sticking out from the edge of the pattern piece, as this makes it difficult to see what you are doing, particularly on small pieces.

Laying out

If the fabric you are intending to use is at all creased, press it thoroughly. Lay it out flat on your cutting-out table, with the selvedge parallel to the edge. Some cutting layouts will show the fabric folded in half, with the selvedges brought together: when doing this, do not try to make the two sides of the folded end of the fabric lie neatly on top of each other, as this may make the folded edge twist or wring. If this happens, open out the fabric and refold it, letting the ends lie where they will.

Lay the pattern pieces on the fabric exactly as shown in the cutting layout you are following. Take great care to keep the grain lines absolutely parallel to the selvedge. Place weights on each pattern piece: books work well. Lay any pattern pieces marked 'lay to fold' with the marked edge up against the fold in

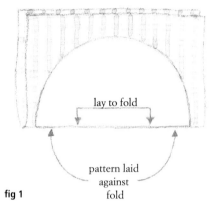

lay to fold

pattern laid against fold

fig 1

the fabric (fig 1). This piece will be cut on the double, so that each half is the mirror image of the other. Once this pattern piece is opened out it will be a single piece, such as the waistcoat back (see page 18). If the fold line is creased, press before beginning to sew any of the seams.

fig 3

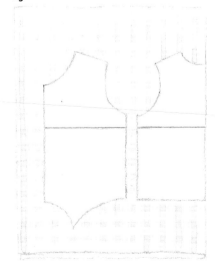

Matching patterns

If you are using checked or any patterned fabric with all but the very smallest motifs, these should match at the seams. Work out which edges on the pattern pieces will be stitched together, lay them side by side and draw a line across them (fig 2).

Lay the pattern pieces on the fabric so that these 'matching' lines lie on exactly the same position on the check or pattern (fig 3). They should then match when stitched together.

For large pattern pieces, such as curtains, measure the 'pattern repeat' and allow that much extra on each drop to ensure a good match.

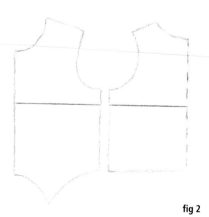

fig 2

Marking and cutting the fabric

Mark around each pattern piece with tailor's chalk or, very lightly, with a soft pencil, taking great care that the pieces do not move and that the pencil doesn't pull the fabric. Test the chalk on a fabric scrap first to ensure that it won't permanently mark the fabric. Mark each notch as you come to it by folding back the edge of the paper and making a tiny mark at right angles to the line. Remove the paper pattern. If the fabric is doubled, put in pins fairly near the edges of each piece to hold the two layers together as you work.

Cut out around each piece carefully: try to cut with long strokes, using the full length of the scissor blades, as this will give a smooth edge. Do not 'nibble' at the fabric with the tips of the scissors, as this will have the opposite effect. Clip not more than 5mm (¼in) into each notch, using the scissor tips.

Bias strips

Bias strips are narrow strips of fabric cut 'on the cross', that is at 45° to the selvedge, which makes them very pliable and stretchy. They are used for binding edges, making piping and bows, or for anything else that requires pliability, either to negotiate curves and corners or to hang softly. If the strips are not cut on the true cross they will tend to twist or wring and look very messy. Small lengths of bias strip can usually be fitted in among the pattern pieces in the layout. Larger quantities – enough for piping a loose cover, for example – can be cut most economically as a separate block, whether the piping is to be made from the main or a contrasting fabric.

Cutting and joining bias strips

1 First find the cross grain: fold the fabric in half lengthways, bringing the selvedges together, and smooth it out. Snip notches through both selvedges, as shown (fig 4).
2 Unfold the fabric and lay it out flat. Mark a straight line between the two notches and cut along it (fig 4).
3 Now fold this cut end up on to the selvedge, patting down the resulting fold until it lies flat (fig 5). Iron the fold lightly, without stretching the fabric.
4 Open the fabric out flat: the crease will now be at 45° to the selvedge, that is on the true cross or bias. Using tailor's chalk or a soft pencil, mark lines on either side of the crease to the required width and cut along them (fig 6).
5 Join bias strips: lay one strip on another, right sides together, strips at right angles (fig 7). Pin and stitch, without stretching, press the seam open (fig 8) and trim off corners.

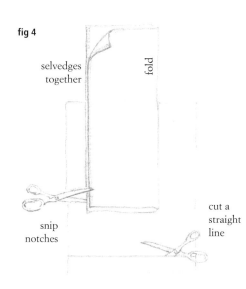

fig 4

selvedges together

fold

snip notches

cut a straight line

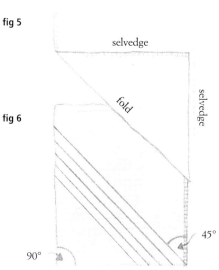

fig 5

selvedge

fold

selvedge

fig 6

90°

45°

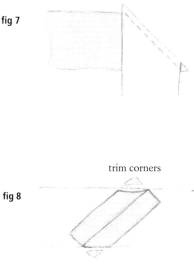

fig 7

trim corners

fig 8

preparing to stitch

Once you have cut out all the pieces, it is only too easy to rush into sewing up everything without thinking about the order in which to do it. This is not a problem with the projects in this book – just follow the instructions in the order they are given. If, however, you are working out a project on your own, you will need to think out each move carefully before you start sewing, so that it is as easy and straightforward as possible. The guidelines below will help you to work out the most practical way in which to make up a project. If you do get it wrong, remember that it is always easier to unpick a seam than to struggle to stitch a fiddly piece with a mass of fabric in the way.

Order of sewing

- Decorations such as pintucking (see page 72) are usually made first.
- Interfacings (see page 34) should almost always be put on before any seams are made.
- As very large pieces of fabric are more cumbersome to manage on the machine, it is best to avoid joining them on until the smaller pieces have been put together. In other words, aim to work with the smallest possible amount of fabric on the machine at each stage.
- Work out what sort of seams you will use, and whether they should be topstitched or piped. If the latter, make the piping first (see pages 82–83).

Pinning

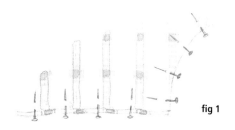

fig 1

Most sewing machines will sew across pins if these are put in at right angles to the stitching line (fig 1); this makes it easier to judge the seam allowance accurately and the pins are easier to remove if all the heads are on the right. Always slow down when stitching over a pin to ensure that the stitch is made across the pin; if the needle hits the pin with force, it will break. Always avoid stitching over pinheads. You can either remove the pins as you stitch or once the seam is completed, but do ensure that they are all removed before beginning the next stage.

Some sewing machines just will not stitch over pins successfully. If yours is one of these, stop and pull out the pins as you come to them. In places where pins are in line with the seam – for example, when setting in a zip – put them in on the stitching line with their heads towards you, so that they are easy to pull out as you come to them.

Tacking

It is not usually necessary to tack. Try stitching the pinned seams (as above). This is quicker, and there are no fiddly bits of thread to pull out afterwards. However, for occasional difficult places, use a contrasting coloured thread and tack just off the stitching line, as this makes it easier to remove the threads after the seam is sewn.

Tacking stitches can be as large as will hold the pieces together until they are sewn. If you are tacking up a garment to try on, make the stitches smaller and include the occasional backstitch so that it will stay together while you put it on.

You can also tack on the sewing machine using the largest stitch: some machines have a long stitch specially for the purpose. Either of these will speed up the job of tacking considerably, although the threads will still have to be unpicked at a later stage.

Seam allowances

fig 2

1.5cm (⅝in)

Except where otherwise specified on the pattern diagrams, these are all 1.5cm (⅝in); this is generally a suitable allowance to use in your own projects as well (fig 2). It is important to stitch seams exactly the specified distance from the cut edge or the pieces will not fit together properly.

Pressing

For a good 'finish', every seam must be pressed before another is sewn across it. To save time, make several seams and press them all at once. Before pressing the seams, experiment on some spare fabric to find the correct heat setting to use.

Stitch length

Most sewing machines have stitch lengths marked from 0 to 4. For most medium-weight fabrics, a setting of 2.5 is about right. Use a longer stitch for heavier fabrics and a shorter stitch for lighter ones. If you use too short a stitch, it may make the seam stiff; too long, and gaps may show on the right side of the fabric. Experience will soon tell you when the stitch length is correct for the fabric you are sewing. Your sewing-machine handbook will tell you how to adjust the tension if your machine is not stitching properly.

Basic stitches

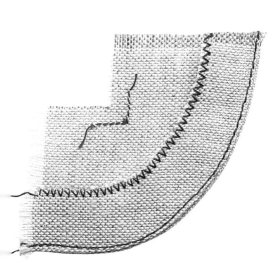

Machine stitches

Straight stitch and backstitch Straight stitch is the basic stitch made by the sewing machine. The size can be adjusted (see above), and most machines will also make this stitch backwards – this is the best way to fasten off seams.

Zigzag This stitch is widely available on modern sewing machines, and is often used for neatening edges (see page 27), making buttonholes, as a decorative edging stitch or for machine embroidery. The size and spacing of the stitches can be adjusted (follow the instructions in your sewing-machine handbook). A slight zigzag should be used for stitching stretch jersey fabrics.

Topstitch In topstitching, instead of the stitches being hidden on the wrong side of the fabric, they are made from the right, or 'top', side usually about 3mm (⅛in) from a finished edge or seam. This technique is used to give a sharp finish to seams, faced or hemmed edges and, if contrasting thread is used, will also provide a decorative touch.

Edge stitch This technique is used to make facings roll on to the wrong side of the fabric and stay there – anyone who has made or worn a garment with facings which insist on flapping over on to the right side will appreciate its merits. For method, see page 35.

Staystitch A straight stitch which is used to prevent weak places tearing or pulling open, and to strengthen edges which might stretch.

Hand stitches

Running stitch and tacking stitch
Running stitch is the basic hand-sewing stitch: take a threaded needle, make a knot in the end and then run the needle in and out of the fabric. As small stitches, it can be used for gathering (see page 70); as long stitches, it becomes tacking (see opposite).

Backstitch This is a very strong stitch. *Take a threaded needle, make a knot in the end, and bring the needle up through the fabric from the wrong to the right side. Make a small stitch forward to the wrong side and another up to the right side. Take a stitch backwards into the end of the first stitch, and come up to the right side a short way ahead. Repeat from * to end.

Slipstitch/Hemstitch Actually one stitch. For method see page 28.

Oversewing A functional stitch used for neatening edges (see page 27).

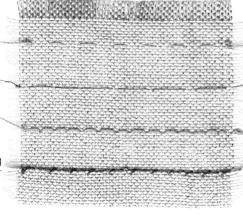

23

Making up

Before starting to sew, indulge yourself by contemplating all the exciting things there are to make: pretty things to decorate your home, or perhaps some simple clothes to give your wardrobe a new look. There are many projects which are easy enough for a newcomer to the craft of sewing to work on successfully.

Try not to be too ambitious at first, and start with the simplest projects while you get used to cutting out, using a sewing machine and all the other things you need to learn at the beginning. This will enable you to build up a library of skills to draw on when you move on to more complex projects.

Always read through all the instructions for a project first, so that you have some idea of how the whole thing fits together. Practise any techniques which are new to you, or seem complicated, on scraps of fabric. Then follow the instructions in the order given to make up your chosen project.

seams

There are two basic seams. Flat seams are the simplest and most useful. They can be used on virtually any fabric, and are the most adaptable to curves and corners. French seams are used mainly with lightweight fabrics where a neat appearance is required on both the wrong and right sides, and for this reason they are the best choice for transparent fabric. They are slightly more complicated to make than flat seams and are difficult to manage on corners and curves. French seams are too bulky to use with heavier fabrics.

Making seams
Flat seams

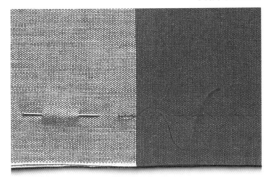

1 Lay the two pieces to be joined with the right sides of the fabric together. Line up the edges one on the other and, with the ends matching, pin the two layers together (see page 22).
2 Place the pinned pieces on the sewing machine, with the edge to be stitched on the right. Slide this edge under the presser foot until the needle is placed exactly the distance specified for the seam allowance from the cut edge, and 5–6mm (¼in) from the end.
3 Lower the presser foot. Using a straight stitch set to reverse, make three or four stitches back to the end of the fabric and then stitch forwards along the seamline, keeping the exact seam allowance. Stitch the seam from pin to pin, repositioning your hands as you go. At the end, make a few backstitches to fasten off.
4 When the edges of the seam have been neatened (see opposite), press the seam open or, where appropriate, to one side. The seam can also be finished with topstitching (see page 23).

French seams

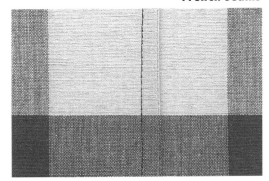

1 Lay the two pieces to be joined with the wrong sides of the fabric together, and with ends and edges matching, as above. For a total seam allowance of 1.5cm (⅝in), pin and stitch as above, 5mm (¼in) from the edge – you will be working on the right side of the fabric in this instance (fig 1).
2 If the cut edge of the seam allowance is uneven or frayed, trim it carefully to give a smooth edge and prevent loose threads sticking out of the finished French seam.
3 From the right side, press the seam allowance carefully to one side. Fold the fabric back neatly through the seam so that the right sides come together, and press again. Do not allow the seam to roll to either side – it should lie exactly on the edge.
4 Working from the wrong side of the fabric, pin and stitch 1cm (⅜in) from the original seam (fig 2).
5 Press the seam allowance carefully to one side (fig 3).

This method makes a neat seam, with the cut edges concealed inside the second row of stitching. The narrower a French seam is, the nicer it will look, so adjust the seam allowance if you wish.

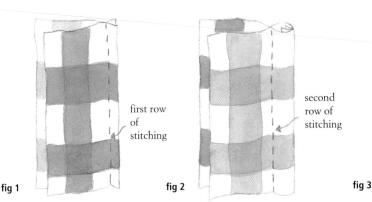

first row of stitching

fig 1

second row of stitching

fig 2

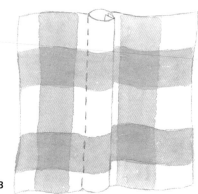

fig 3

Neatening edges

fig 4a
zigzag

fig 4b
turned over edge

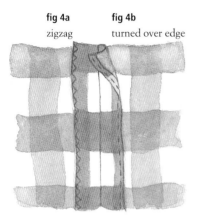

fig 5

There are three ways of neatening, or 'finishing', edges.

1 Stitch with zigzag so that one side of the stitch goes over the edge of the fabric (fig 4a). Adjust the size of the stitch so that it is open and wide enough to cover several threads of the fabric, making a finish that will not fray. If the zigzag stitch stiffens the edge, experiment with a wider stitch spacing. This is the most practical finish for home sewing and, if done carefully, is neat enough to use whenever the wrong side of the fabric will not normally be seen. It is easier to do this before pressing the seams open, and the two edges can be zigzagged either separately or together.

2 On thinner fabrics, the edge can be turned over on to the wrong side by approximately 5mm (¼in) and stitched using straight stitch (fig 4b). It is easier to do this without pinning or pressing. It makes a neat edge to use if the inside will be visible, as in an unlined curtain.

3 If your machine cannot do zigzag stitch, oversewing the edges by hand will prevent fraying (fig 5), although unless you are a neat stitcher it will not look as good as a machine-stitched edge. Giant-sized oversewing is sometimes the only remedy for extra-thick or openweave fabrics which fray easily, since a zigzag stitch may catch only one or two threads and this is not enough to prevent the edge of the fabric from pulling away when in use.

Strategies for better seams

● Always stitch a test seam on a fabric remnant or offcut. Alter the stitch length until the stitching is completely smooth. If the seam puckers, try altering the stitch tension (the bobbin tension seldom needs altering).

● Notches indicate which pieces of fabric go where and how they fit together, so do match them accurately.

● Backstitch both ends of every seam, otherwise they may start to unravel and weaken the seam. Trim off thread ends which could catch in the machine.

● Use good quality thread, poor thread tends to stretch or break.

● Make sure that both sides of a seam are the same length before pinning or tacking. If not, check why and remedy it (see page 29, Stitching curved seams).

● Some fabrics stretch easily. To counteract this, stitch narrow tape into all seams which will have any strain placed on them.

● Too much pressure on the presser foot may cause seams to stretch; too little, and the fabric will not move through the machine properly.

● When sewing pile fabrics such as velvet, the top layer tends to slide, or 'walk', over the under layer. If the seam is tacked, this will cause small tucks to form along its length; if pinned, one layer will end up longer than the other. To remedy this, first either put the pins in at right angles to the seam and closer together than usual, or tack firmly. Then, holding the fabric in front of the machine with the right hand and behind with the left, pull your hands gently apart, thus 'tensioning' the fabric. Do not stretch it. Stitch the seam, allowing the fabric to pass through the machine at the same rate as the stitches are made, pulling neither from front nor back. Work from pin to pin, repositioning your hands each time.

● Using a larger stitch, plus tensioning, may also help to remedy stretching.

hems

A well stitched hand-sewn hem is practically invisible but machine-sewn hems are stronger, rarely come down and can give a crisp, neat finish. Lined curtains, however, are always hemmed by hand, and delicate or very smooth fabrics, such as satin, usually look better with a hand-sewn hem. Otherwise, it is simply a matter of taste, so use whichever you prefer.

Straight hems

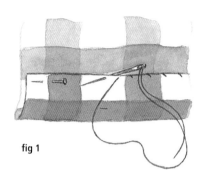

fig 1

1 Lay the edge to be hemmed on the ironing board, with the wrong side facing upwards. Start by turning a short length of the fabric over on to the wrong side by the amount allowed for the hem (for example, 5cm/2in). Press, then turn up the next piece and press again, continuing in this way until the whole length of the hem has been pressed. Aim for a smooth line rather than sticking to the exact hem measurement, particularly at seams.

2 If you are making a garment, pin the hem in place and try it on. Adjust, pin, and re-press if necessary. For other items, hang or lay out the whole hem and check that it looks even. Adjust, pin and re-press if necessary.

3 Unpin and trim the hem allowance, making it all the same depth again.

4 Neaten the edge of the hem, using whichever method is most appropriate (see page 27) and bearing in mind that zigzag stitch will cut down on bulk on thicker fabrics. Press the neatened edge and re-press the folded edge if necessary. On hems which will be hand sewn, avoid pressing across the neatened edge as this may leave an impression on the right side.

5 Machine-sewn hems can be stitched from the right or wrong side, although if the fabric is checked or striped it is obviously easier to a follow a line in the pattern from the right side. In this case, use the pins both to hold the hem in place and as a stitching guide on the edge of the hem. When working from the wrong side, the pins can be put in at right angles to the edge. Hand-sewn hems are always pinned and stitched from the wrong side of the garment.

For a machine-sewn hem:

6 Stitch the hem close to the neatened edge, backstitching or overlapping the stitches at each end, as appropriate. It is sometimes useful to tension the fabric (see page 27), which will usually prevent any puckering. Press.

For a hand-sewn hem:

6 Using slipstitch or hemstitch (fig 1) and a long thread, work from the wrong side. Fasten the thread firmly on the neatened edge. Stitch into the main fabric, picking up only one or two threads (stitches should not be visible on the right side). Stitch back into the hem edge, taking a slightly larger stitch.

Continue from side to side, keeping the stitches even and fairly close together, and being careful not to pull them tight as you sew. Press.

Decorative finishes

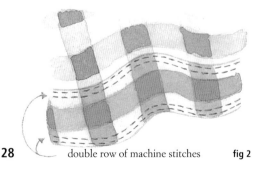

double row of machine stitches   fig 2

• Machined hems look nicer if they are stitched close to both the free edge and the folded edge. This is often done with double rows of stitches (fig 2).

• If fabric without an obvious right or wrong side is being used, the hem can be reversed by turning it up on to the right side.

• Facings can be used instead of hems if a decorative finish is required. Fabric of a contrasting colour or texture can be used, or lining if the main fabric is bulky (see page 35 for how to cut a facing). The facing can either be set on in the usual way or in reverse and turned up to form a band on the right side. The free end should then be topstitched in place.

• Self and contrast piping or other decorative edgings can be let into faced hems to add a further dimension; for example, try a check fabric piping with a matching plain-coloured fabric.

curves

Curved seams are made in a similar way to straight seams but are more difficult to put together accurately. This section explains how to use the special methods which have evolved to overcome the various problems which you may encounter.

Using curved seams

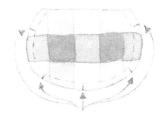

fig 3   notches

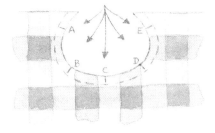

Curved seams are used in two places:
- Decoratively, for instance when a circle is set into a surrounding piece, such as the centrepiece for a cushion.
- To shape the fabric to fit around curves and shaped edges. In this case, one side of the seam is sometimes cut longer than the other (step 2 below).

Stitching curved seams

1 Pin the corresponding pairs of notches together (fig 3), starting at one end.
2 If the fabric between two pairs of notches is longer on one side than on the other, it must be gathered, or 'gauged', to fit (see page 70). Make gathering stitches and draw up to fit.
3 Pin the seam with the pins at right angles to the edge.
4 Stitch the seam, being careful to take

the correct seam allowance. This is sometimes quite fiddly on tight curves, so take your time. If gathers have been used, it is easier to stitch the seam with the flat side on top.

Perfect fitting is possible with careful pinning, accurate seam allowances and matching of notches, so do use them – they are not there for decoration!

Remember:
- It is the stitching lines which must match, not the edges.
- The two sides may not match properly if the wrong amount is taken for the seam allowance.
- A curved seam will be partly on the straight grain and partly off it, and the latter parts will therefore tend to stretch as you stitch. See page 27 for how to counteract this.

Making seam allowances lie flat

On the inside of a curve the seam allowance will be full and form waves, while on the outside of the curve it will be too small to lie flat. The tighter the curve, the more pronounced the effect.
1 Press the seam allowance on the inside edge flat, making triangular folds if necessary to take in the fullness (fig 4).

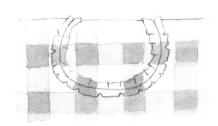

fig 4

2 Clip the seam allowance on the outside edge in towards the stitching. These clips will open out and enable the allowance to lie flat (fig 4). On tight curves it is often necessary to clip within a thread or two of the stitching, so if there will be any strain on the seam sew a row of staystitches over the original row to strengthen it.

Curved hems

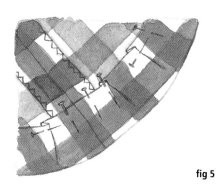

fig 5

A curved hem presents problems because of the extra fullness that appears when the edge is turned up.
1 The tighter the curve, the narrower the hem should be cut, thus reducing the fullness.
2 Try shrinking the cut edge by pressing with a steam iron.
3 If any surplus remains (or a wider hem is required), make small tucks on the edge to reduce it. Do this on the ironing board with the hem turned up, so that you can see exactly where the fullness

lies naturally and make the tucks in those places only (fig 5). To avoid lumps, make the tucks slightly away from the seams.
4 Slipstitch or machine as for straight hems. If the former, make a backstitch to hold each tuck in place.
5 Sometimes the most practical way to finish a curved hem is to face it, (see opposite), using the same fabric or a thinner one, and to add to this effect it can be set on so that the facing lies on the right side.

corners

You will sometimes need to make neat flat corners or points, for example on the front of collars or on the Rabbit-eared cushion on page 58. For these, and for making mitres, a good technique ensures a satisfactory finish.

Making corners and points

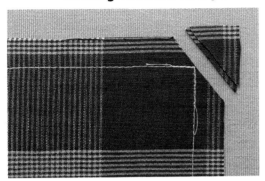

1 Lay the main fabric piece and its facing (see page 34) with right sides together and pin. Sometimes the facing piece is cut marginally smaller to encourage the seams to roll to the wrong side: in this case, make sure to keep the edges absolutely together when pinning.

2 Machine stitch up to the corner and, keeping the needle in the fabric, lift the presser foot, swing the fabric round so that the foot faces along the second side, lower the foot, and continue stitching to the end.

3 Stitch a row of small staystitches on top of the first stitches for 2–3cm (1in) on each side of the corner to reinforce the seam and prevent fraying around the point once the fabric is trimmed.

4 Trim back the fabric around the point, right up against the double line of stitching. This can be a bit frightening at first, but must be done! The sharper the point, the more fabric must be trimmed.

5 Turn the fabric right side out and, if you have cut enough away, you will be rewarded with a sharp corner. Press firmly from the wrong side. If the corner does not lie flat or looks lumpy, you have not trimmed off enough fabric. If the corner is narrower than a right angle, it may be necessary to push a blunt knitting needle or similar tool into it to turn it out properly; do this gently to avoid going through the fabric.

Mitres

Mitres are useful for such things as the outer edges of a pillowcase or when 'framing' a piece of embroidery to use on a cushion. Cut four strips to form the frame, each one longer than the outside measurement of the frame to allow for cutting the corners. When making pieces of a specified size it is easier to make a paper pattern first.

Making mitres

1 Cut two pieces of fabric to the required width, including a seam allowance on each side. When sewing small pieces, make the seam allowance narrower than normal: 1cm (⅜in) is usually all you need.

2 Fold the end to be mitred to lie accurately along the adjacent side and make a crease to mark the line for the mitre. Repeat for the second strip but at the opposite end, so that the two strips will form a right angle (fig 1).

3 Unfold the strips, add a seam allowance beyond the crease line and cut off the corners.

4 Lay the two pieces one on the other, with right sides together (fig 2). Pin and stitch, and then press the seam open (fig 3). When stitching, use accurate seam allowances, avoid stretching the seam and trim away seam allowance bulk.

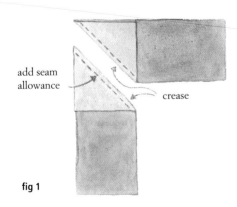

add seam allowance

crease

30   fig 1

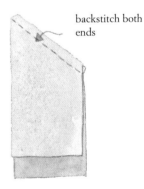

backstitch both ends

fig 2

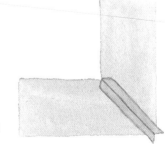

fig 3

lapping seams

Lapping is really an alternative method of making seams, where instead of being sewn from the inside they are stitched from the top or right side (topstitching). This technique is especially useful for tightly curved or angled seams. It is also an easy way of making seams cut on the bias, both because you can see what you are doing and because the seam will not stretch so easily when stitched in this way. Lapping is widely used for appliqué and other kinds of decorative sewing.

Lapping corners

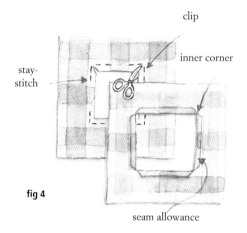

clip

inner corner

stay-stitch

fig 4

seam allowance

There are two methods, depending on whether the seam allowance is on the inside or outside of the corner to be lapped over another piece.

1 Cut out a square frame shape, as shown in fig 4. From other fabrics, cut out a small square that will overlap the centre of the frame by at least 5cm (2in) all round, and a large square, at least 8cm (3in) larger than the outer dimensions of the frame.

2 For inside corners, staystitch approximately 2cm (¾in) around both sides of each inner corner, about 1 cm (⅜in) from the edge. Clip into the corners and press the seam allowance

accurately on to the wrong side (fig 4).

3 Lay this, right side up, centrally on to the small square and pin in place on the inner edge (fig 5). Machine stitch all round, 5mm (¼in) from the edge. At the corners, leave the needle in the fabric, lift the presser foot, turn the fabric so that the foot faces along the adjacent side, lower the foot and continue.

4 For outside corners, press the outer edges of the 'frame' on to the wrong side, folding a 1cm (⅜in) seam allowance neatly at the corners (fig 6).

5 Lay centrally on to the large square, pin in place and stitch as above, 5mm (¼in) from the outer edge (fig 7).

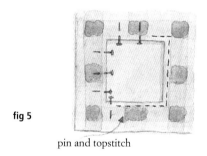

fig 5

pin and topstitch

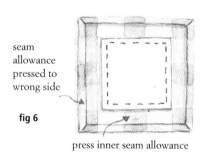

seam allowance pressed to wrong side

fig 6

press inner seam allowance

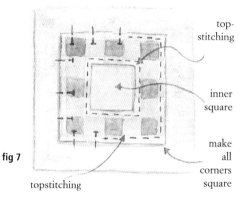

top-stitching

inner square

make all corners square

fig 7

topstitching

Lapping curves

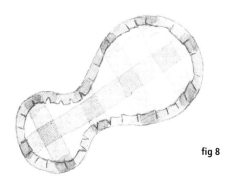

fig 8

1 Carefully press the seam allowance on the piece that will lap over the top on to the wrong side.

2 Where the seam allowance is on the outside of the curve, clip in to it as you press, to allow it to lie flat. The clips should be made closer and deeper on very tight curves than on shallower ones, although they must never go right across the allowance (fig 8).It is easiest to do all this directly on the ironing

board and, working from the wrong side, press slowly and carefully round all the edges.

3 Where the seam allowance is on the inside of the curve, it will be too full to lie flat, so press it into small, triangular tucks.

4 Pin the piece in position from the right side, with the pressed edges neatly lapping over the edges of the other piece, and topstitch.

31

billowing curtain

This curtain for a French window is made from cotton organdie, a fabric with lots of 'bounce' that adds to the billowing effect created by the unusual cut. Organdie is an easy fabric both to cut and sew as it is crisp and does not stretch easily; however, it is important on these curved seams to be very careful not to pull on the fabric as this might stretch the seams. As organdie is the same on both sides, there are no right and wrong sides to worry about. Other fabrics could be used so long as they have some of the bounce needed to encourage the billows. Starched voile or muslin would give a similar effect, but would also need a wider and closer zigzag to prevent fraying: the curtain is made almost entirely with zigzag stitch, both to finish the lapped seams and all the edges. Thread in various colours – pale blues, greens and turquoises in the curtain shown – is used on the right side. There is no need to change the bobbin thread colour to match, simply use white throughout.

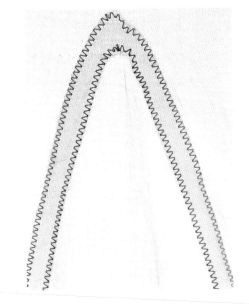

You will need

For a curtain 2.4m (8ft) long:
5.50m (6¼yd) organdie, 112cm (44in) wide
Sewing thread in shades of pale blue, green, turquoise, grey and white
10m (11yd) white cotton tape
Metre rule (yardstick), HB pencil

To cut out

1 Press the fabric. Using the diagrams on pages 98–99, cut the main fabric piece to the size shown and lightly draw in the three lines for the slits and the marker line for the heading, using an HB pencil and a metre rule (yardstick). Cut the slits only (not the marker line), taking great care to make the cuts smooth and exactly the same length.
2 Scale up the pattern for the triangular insets from the diagram and use it to cut out three triangles of fabric. Also cut out two side strips and one rectangle for the heading to the sizes shown.

Lapping seams and making points

Before starting to make up the curtain, you will need to practise making lapped zigzag seams and points.
1 Adjust the machine to make a small, fairly open zigzag stitch, close enough to neaten the edges but not so close that it stretches or stiffens the seams.
2 Using spare scraps of fabric, lap one straight edge 2cm (¾in) over another and stitch two rows 1cm (⅜in) apart and 1–2mm (¹⁄₁₆in) from the cut edges. Trim

the edges as described opposite.
3 Again using spare scraps of fabric, cut a slit in one and a point in another using the inset pattern, and then practise stitching around the point as described below. Although the points are not difficult to make, they are fiddly, so do practise on small pieces first.

To make up

1 Lay the top of one of the slits in the main piece over one of the insets, so that it lies in the centre and about 2cm (¾in) below the point. Pin in place.
2 Lap one edge of the slit 2cm (¾in) over one edge of the inset and pin down to the bottom. Pin the second side in the same way (fig 1).
3 Using a coloured thread and changing it at random during the stitching, start at the bottom and with the main piece on top, stitch 1–2mm (¹⁄₁₆in) in from the cut edge, curving in slightly to the point. Leave the needle in the fabric, lift the presser foot and turn the fabric so that

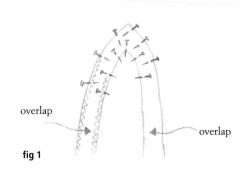

overlap

overlap

fig 1

machine, it is extremely resilient and it will spring back to life once pressed.

4 Working with the main piece, lay a selvedge on top of one of the side strips, matching the edges. Pin along the selvedge and the inner edge of the strip. Stitch twice as on the insets, the first row just inside the selvedge and the second on the inner edge of the strip. Trim all the edges, cutting off the selvedges. Finish the other side of the main piece in exactly the same way.

5 Press the heading in half lengthways, and on one long edge press 2cm (¾in) of fabric on to the inside. Open it out and lay the unpressed edge on the curtain so that it lies along the marker line. Pin and stitch with long straight stitches (fig 2).

6 Press the heading to lie on the top part of the curtain, lapping the free pressed edge over on to the wrong side and pinning it in place along the row of straight stitches (put these pins in from the right side of the curtain and at right angles to the seam). From the right side and reverting to zigzag, stitch close to the seam and again 1cm (⅜in) above it.

fig 2

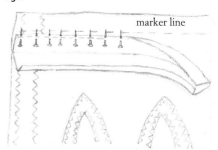

marker line

the foot is facing down the second side. Lower the foot and stitch to the bottom. On the other side of the overlap, stitch a second row parallel to and about 1cm (⅜in) from the first, again curving round at the top. Using small, very sharp and highly pointed scissors, trim the two cut edges close to the stitches. Insert the other two insets in the same way.

Although the organdie will crease as it is turned and squeezed through the

Make two rows of zigzag close to the top edge as before.

7 Sew pairs of tapes to the wrong side of the seam below the top, from which to hang the curtain.

8 To make the hem, turn up and press 4cm (1½in) of fabric on to the wrong side. Stitch close to the cut edge and again 1cm (⅜in) below this. Trim the cut edge. Press the curtain and tie the tapes to rings or directly onto a pole.

facings, interfacings & linings

Many people confuse these three categories, so here are explanations as to what they are, where they are used and how to use them.

A facing is a piece of fabric stitched to a free edge to finish or hide it, in a similar way to a hem. Unlike a hem, however, a facing can also be used to finish tightly curved edges or where there are corners or angles.

As the name implies, interfacing comes between the facing and the outer layer. The names interfacing, interlining and backing are interchangeable, although the last also refers to much stiffer fabrics such as those used to back pelmets.

Linings usually cover most of the inside of outer garments and curtains, protecting against wear and fading, and providing warmth and ease of movement.

Facings

Facings, unlike hems, can be used to 'finish' edges which are not straight, whether tightly curved or angled. They are, usually, narrow strips of fabric cut to exactly the same shape as the edges they will face. They are usually cut from the main fabric, but can also be cut from fabrics in contrasting colours or textures to add decoration, from thinner fabric to avoid bulk, or from heavier fabric to encourage an edge to hang well. Facings for such things as tabs and tie-backs are usually cut from cotton lining fabric.

Interfacings

Interfacings are used to prevent edges stretching and impressions of the seam showing on the right side of the fabric. They are also used to strengthen the area interfaced, for instance where ties or other fastenings will be stitched on. Interfacings can be cut from materials specifically made for the purpose, such as the bonded (non-woven), fusible (iron-on) fabrics that are widely available in many different weights. These fabrics have the advantage of not fraying and are usually designed to be washable. Alternatively, interfacings can be made from calico, lawn and muslin.

The weight and stiffness of the interfacing should relate to that of the main fabric and the outcome required: if you are making a pelmet, you may require interfacing as stiff as a board, but for an embroidered pillowcase, either muslin or featherweight bonded interfacing might be a better choice.

Wadding or padded interfacings can be used to create a quilted effect or for insulation. Think about the effect you want to achieve and choose a fabric which, when combined with the outer fabric, will accomplish this. Most bonded interfacings are much stiffer after they have been applied, so make allowance for this when buying one.

Linings

Linings should generally have a slippery surface so that they move easily against another fabric. It is generally best to use the fabrics made specifically for the purpose, although try to find one which is pliable and not stiff, which so many of the cheaper ones are. For lined curtains, cotton sateen or 'curtain lining' is generally the best choice, as it is soft and pliable and can be washed.

Washing

If linings and facings are to be sewn into an item which will be washed, ensure that they, too, are washable. However, as they may have different rates of shrinkage, they should be washed before being cut out. Even if curtains or loose covers are washable it is often more practical to have them dry cleaned as they are usually large and can be unwieldy to iron.

Patterns

Linings are cut from the pattern used for the outer part of the item, with adjustments to allow for facings and hems. For both facings and interfacings, separate patterns are made from the relevant parts of the main pattern. The circular tablecloth which appears as a detail on page 8 has a facing cut from plain fabric.

Making and using a simple facing pattern

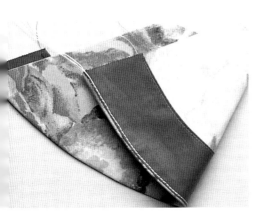

1 Lay the pattern pieces to be faced on a sheet of paper (fig 1). Draw around the cut edges to be faced, marking any notches clearly if there are any.

2 Remove the pattern. Decide how wide the facing should be and draw the inner edge onto the paper. Cut out the facing pattern piece (fig 2).

3 Cut the facing from the fabric and interfacing if required.

4 Lay the pieces of interfacing in place: fusible interfacing should be fused to facing pieces, sewn-in interfacings attached to main pieces by pinning and stitching on the outer edges only.

5 Stitch all the seams on both the main pieces and on the facings, trim any loose threads and press them open.

6 On the main piece, neaten the seams (see page 27), except where the facings will cover them. Also neaten the free edges of the facings.

7 With right sides together, lay the facings on the main piece, carefully matching the edges, notches, seams and ends, and pin in place.

8 Stitch all round, taking the correct seam allowance and backstitching at each end or overlapping the stitches, whichever is appropriate.

Then either edge stitch the facing:

9 Fold the facing to lie over the seam allowance. Do not press the seam.

10 From the right side, and holding the facing so that it does not roll over the seam, stitch on the facing close to the seam line (1–3mm/$\frac{1}{16}$–$\frac{1}{8}$in, depending on the weight of the fabric) and through on to the seam allowance below.

11 Clip the seam allowance where necessary to allow it to lie flat. Do not clip the stitches – just up to them.

12 Fold the facing on to the wrong side. The seam will now roll on to the wrong side and stay there, holding the facing in place and giving a very neat finish. Press the edge lightly.

More than any other technique, edge stitching will help to avoid the home-made look, so it is well worth devoting some time to learning it.

• Edge stitching can be used on most facings but is difficult on some small, fiddly pieces as the sewing machine cannot get right into the corners. In this case, sew up as close as possible to the corner, backstitch, then jump the corner and start again as near to it as possible.

• In places where the facing will be turned back (as on revers), it is usual either not to edge stitch or to do it on the reverse, so that the seam will roll over to the side which will not be seen.

Or instead of edge stitching:

9 With the wrong side up, fold the seam allowance over the facing and clip into it to allow it to lie flat.

10 With the right side up, press the facing back sharply to lie over the seam allowance. Do not allow it to roll over the seam.

11 Fold the facing on to the wrong side, rolling the seam to lie on the inside. Press firmly, using a damp cloth laid between the iron and the facing.

fold circle into quarters

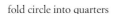

mark on paper

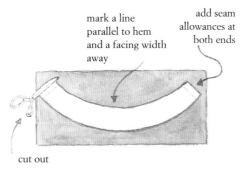

mark a line parallel to hem and a facing width away

add seam allowances at both ends

cut out

fig1

fig 2

cloth & napkins

These two very simple projects are good ones to start with if you have not sewn much before. Both are made up with straight machine stitching, so are good practice with the sewing machine. All the edges are finished by machine so they are quick to make.

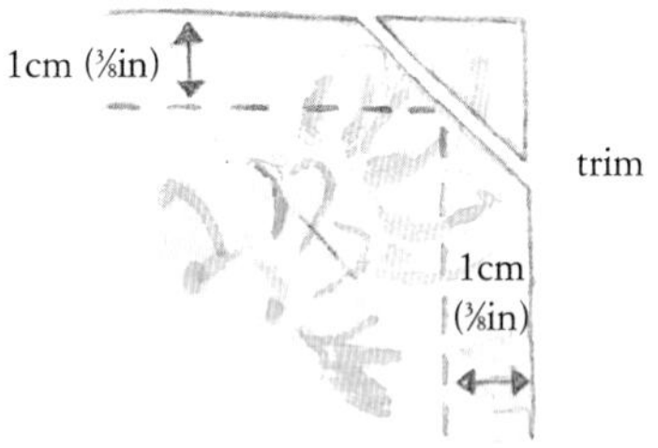

You will need

For a tablecloth 116cm (46in) square:
1.2m (48in) cotton or linen fabric,
    120cm (48in) wide
For four napkins 28cm (11in) square:
30cm (12in) cotton or linen fabric,
    120cm (48in) wide
Matching sewing thread

To make up

1 Press the fabric for the tablecloth and lay it out flat. Using a set square, check that the cut ends are at right angles to the selvedges and trim if necessary. Trim the edge off the selvedges.
2 Press the fabric for the napkins, trim the selvedges and, using a set square, cut into four equal squares.
3 Trim the corners on all five pieces (fig 1). Press 1cm (⅜in) of fabric over on to the wrong side on each edge.
4 Stitch all round each piece as close to the outer edge as possible.
5 Press a further 2cm (¾in) of fabric over on to the wrong side, folding the corners neatly. Pin in place, with the pins at right angles to the edge.
6 Stitch all round, this time close to the inner edge of the hem.
7 Press the tablecloth and all four napkins from the wrong side, using plenty of steam.

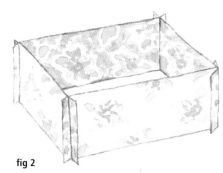

1cm (⅜in)

trim

1cm (⅜in)

fig1

---

basket lining

Lining a plain basket to turn it into a picnic basket is an easy project which would make a delightful wedding present. Use a pretty floral cotton like the one shown in the picture – a plasticized cotton is practical, while quilted cotton would insulate the food.

You will need

Fabric – this basket lining takes very little fabric, so would offer a good opportunity to use up remnants; otherwise, work out the amount required from the measurements of your own basket
Matching sewing thread

To cut out

1 Measure the length and width of the base and the height of the sides, inside the basket. The sides can be made in one long piece or as four separate pieces, as best fits the fabric.
2 Mark out the pieces on the wrong side of the fabric, adding seam allowances all round the base and to three sides of the side pieces. Also add a hem allowance to the fourth side (the top) of the side pieces. Cut out.
3 Cut four pieces of fabric for the ties, each 30 x 4cm (12 x 1½in).

To make up

1 Make the ties. Fold each piece of fabric in half lengthways (right side out) and press. Fold and press each side in half again (to inside). Fold in one end and press. Stitch close to pressed edges.
2 Make the lining sides:
● If they are cut from one piece, fold the ends to lie right sides together, pin, stitch and neaten the edges.
● If they are cut from four pieces, join them into a ring (fig 2) and neaten.
3 Neaten one long edge and press the hem on to the wrong side. Tuck the un-neatened end of a tie under the hem at each corner and pin in place (fig 3). Stitch the hem, backstitch over the ties.
4 Lay the lower edge of the sides on the base, right sides together, then pin and stitch all round. Press the seam to lie under the base and topstitch all round.
5 Put the lining in the basket, thread the ties through at the corners and knot.

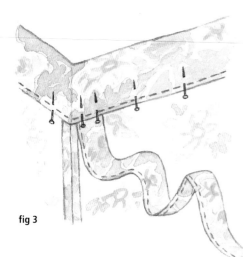

fig 2

fig 3

windbreak

The smaller windbreak made here has three poles and closed casings for easy carrying.

You will need

2 x 2m (2¼yd) strong fabric, 137cm (54in) wide, in two different designs
Strong sewing thread
3 wooden poles, diameter 3cm (1¼in), each 1.5m (5ft) long
Craft knife
Metre rule (yardstick)

To make up

1 Trim the two pieces of fabric, making sure that the corners are square and clipping all the notches (see fig1).
2 Make a point at one end of each pole using a craft knife.
3 Lay the two pieces of fabric right sides together, pin, and then stitch both ends and one long side with a 2cm (¾in) seam allowance. Stitch the second long side between the notches for the casings (not across the casings), leaving an opening about 12cm (5in) long on one side. Turn right side out through the opening. Press.
4 Slipstitch the opening closed and machine stitch across the closed ends of each of the casings, close to the edge, to reinforce them.
5 Using tailor's chalk and a metre rule (yardstick), mark lines between the notches for the casings on one of the pieces of fabric (fig 1). Pin the two layers together through these lines and stitch, backstitching firmly at each end.
6 Slide the blunt end of the poles into the slots and roll up, ready for use.

fig 1

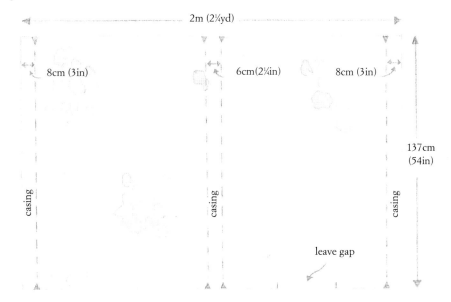

2m (2¼yd)

8cm (3in)   6cm (2¼in)   8cm (3in)

137cm (54in)

casing   casing   casing

leave gap

39

backed curtain swag

Decorate a window with this pretty draped swag. Choose two complementary curtain fabrics, as both sides will show when the swag is hanging at the window. As the swag must be made to fit the window, no specific measurements can be given, but it is easy to work them out following the instructions given below. The swag is also simple both to cut out and to make up.

You will need

Main fabric and lining (see To measure up and To cut out)
2 hooks, large enough to hold bunched-up swag at corners
Matching sewing thread
Long piece of string
1m (1yd) strong tape for ties

To measure up

1 Using fig 1 as a guide, take the measurements A, B and C (as described in steps 2 and 3) and draw them on to a diagram of the shape shown in fig 2.
2 To find lengths A and B, take a long piece of string and form it into a loop in the top of the window from corner to corner, allowing it to drop down to the depth required for the swag. Measure the depth, double it to allow for the folds and mark it on as B. Measure the string used for the loop plus the extra lengths hanging at each side to give the length for side A.
3 Measure the width of the window and add on twice the full length that the swag will hang down on each side for C.
4 Add seam allowances all round the edge of the shape in fig 2.

To cut out

1 Using fig 2 as a guide and working on the wrong side of the main fabric, draw out the shape using tailor's chalk or a pencil and cut out. Repeat for the lining, remembering to turn the pattern over. If the window is large, it may be necessary to make joins in the fabric before cutting.

To make up

1 With right sides together, lay the main piece and lining one on the other and pin. Stitch all round, leaving a gap large enough for the swag to be turned easily out through it.
2 Turn the swag right side out and press all round the edges. Slipstitch the gap closed.

To hang

1 Fix hooks securely at the corners of the window.
2 Form the swag into three folds as shown in fig 3. Measure the distance between hooks (D) and mark centrally on uppermost fold. Cut tape into two ties and stitch centre of each tie on to marked points to match up with hooks.
3 Tie tapes to the hooks and adjust the swag to fall into pleasing drapes.

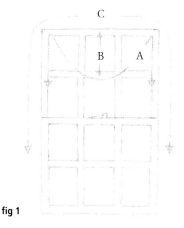

fig 1

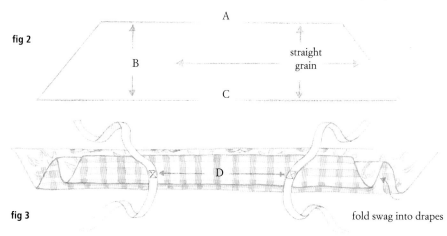

fig 2

fig 3

fold swag into drapes

garden pavilion

Combine simple woodworking with sewing to make this unusual pavilion and add a dashing air to the garden in summer. If necessary, team up with a friend with complementary woodworking skills to avoid taking on too many new things at once. The pavilion is easy to put up and quick to dismantle. Either use different fabrics on each side as in the picture, or make it all from one fabric.

Pavilion cover

You will need

13.5 (15½ yd) strong furnishing fabric,
   or canvas, 150cm (60in) wide
4m tape, for ties
Strong sewing thread
4 large eyelets

To cut out

Following the cutting layout on page
100, and using measurements in figs 1
and 2, cut out: 4 triangular pieces, for
the roof; 4 valance pieces; 3 side pieces;
1 door; 2 side fronts; 1 pennant

To make up

1 Zigzag the edges of all the fabric
pieces (except any which will be sewn
with French seams, see below).
2 Make the four valances: on each
piece, press the seam allowance to the
wrong side on the short ends and
curved side. Topstitch 1cm (⅜in) from
the pressed edges.
3 Lay one roof piece on another, with
right sides together, matching short
edges. Pin, and then stitch, starting 2cm
(¾in) above the lower edge and ending
4cm (1½in) below the apex. Repeat for
the other three sides.
4 Lay the long side of a valance on the
lower edge of one of the roof pieces,
with right sides together, matching
edges and ends. Pin and stitch. Press the
seam allowance to lie under the roof.
Repeat for the other three pieces.
5 Measure the length between the
studding on the roof horizontals (see the
frame opposite) and fix an eyelet in all
four corners of the roof, through the
seams, so that they fit over.
6 Lay a side front on a side piece, with
right sides together, matching the long
edges and notches. Pin and stitch. Press
the seam to one side and topstitch
(alternatively, these seams could be
made with French seams, see page 26,

to give a neater finish inside the tent).
Stitch on the other two side pieces in
the same way and finally stitch on
second side front.
7 Press the hem on to the wrong side of
the fabric, pin and stitch close to the
neatened edge. Finish the straight edges
of the side fronts in the same way. Hem
all around the sides and the lower edge
of the door.
8 Lap the top edges of the side fronts
over the top edge of the door, leaving a
38cm (15in) gap in the middle. Pin and
stitch close to the top.
9 Lap the seam joining the valances to
the roof over the top edge of the sides
and door by 3cm (1in), matching seams
and corners. Pin in place. Topstitch all
round twice, once close to the original
seam and once 2cm (¾in) above it.
10 Sew tapes, in pairs, inside the long
seams to tie around uprights.
11 Make a turning on the two long
edges of the pennant. Neaten the short
end and turn enough over to the wrong
side to make a channel to fit the
studding. Pin and stitch.
12 Follow steps 11 and 12 opposite, to
fit the cover on the frame.

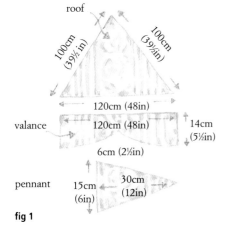

fig 1

fig 2

Note: the pavilion sides
are 190cm (75in) long

The frame

You will need

Tools

Tenon saw; drill; screwdriver; hammer; vice; tape measure; set square and protractor

Materials

4 wooden poles, diameter 3cm (1⅛in), each 183cm (72in) long, for uprights

4 wooden poles, diameter 2.5cm (1in), each 112cm (44in) long, for roof horizontals

4 wooden poles, diameter 2.5cm (1in), each 94cm (37in) long, for apex poles

8 pieces 8mm (⅜in) diameter studding (threaded steel rod), each 8cm (3in) long, and 1 piece 23cm (9in) long

6 wing nuts and washers, to fit studding

1 nut, to fit studding

16 small right-angled steel brackets (each side 4–5 cm (1½ –2in) long), with two holes in each side

Box of 20mm (¾in) no 6 screws

10m (33ft) strong cord, for guy ropes

4 tent pegs

See page 101 for construction diagrams.

To make up

1 Drill 2cm (¾in) deep holes into both ends of the uprights, and screw one of the short pieces of studding into each hole so that 6cm (2½in) protrudes.

2 Flatten eight of the metal brackets completely, using a vice and hammer.

3 Using the saw, cut slots in each end of the horizontal poles to half the depth of the flattened brackets (detail, page 101).

4 Push one end of a flattened bracket into a slot, then slide it out sideways until you can see the holes, mark the positions on the pole (detail, page 101).

5 Lay the pole flat with the slot horizontal. Drill holes centrally through the top half only.

6 Push bracket back into the pole and screw through both to anchor. Repeat at each end of the four roof horizontals.

7 Using the vice, open out the other brackets to 145° (see template, page 100). Fix these into each end of the apex poles in the same way as above, ensuring that the brackets in each end of a pole bend in opposite directions.

8 Spike the uprights into the ground and fix the horizontals in place by slipping the outer holes in the brackets over the studding (main diagram page 101).

9 Fix the four apex poles together at one end by threading the 23cm (9in) piece of studding through the outer holes in the brackets. Secure above and below with a washer and wing nut.

10 Slip an outer hole in the bracket on the end of each apex pole over the studding on one of the uprights, and screw a washer and wing nut on top.

11 Remove the wing nuts from the frame, drop the cover over it and replace the wing nuts again. Push the long studding through the apex hole, slide on the pennant and fix with the nut. Adjust the uprights to the required angle.

12 Cut the cord into four and knot one end of each piece. From inside the pavilion, thread the unknotted ends through the eyelets to the outside. Knock in the tent pegs and tie the cords to them.

Fastenings

Using fastenings is vital for dressmaking; all but the simplest shift needs some sort of fastening, from a single button to a pair of ties or a zip. In home sewing there are plenty of attractive items which require no fastenings at all: pillowcases, tablecloths, curtains – even chair covers, which can simply be fitted in place and stitched up. But with a choice of fastenings available, projects can be adapted or decorated to suit your own home. Use ties on curtains, with squab cushions or on bags, add buttons to decorate cushions or pillowcases or to finish bolsters, and use zips for practical fastenings on cushions and loose covers.

On the following pages you will discover how to make and use lacing, ties, buttons and buttonholes, as well as how to set in zips easily, neatly and quickly. Decorative variations are also included to use as embellishments on otherwise plain pieces of work.

zips &
eyelets

Zips are useful where no other fastening would be satisfactory: in the side of a close-fitting dress, for example, a zip – unlike buttoning or lacing – would give a completely smooth line. Zips are cheap and quick to set in, but are usually hidden away as they do not look particularly attractive, although on sports and casual clothes zips have come to be accepted as a design feature. In soft furnishings their use is limited mainly to cushions and loose covers. Eyelets are less frequently used, but are the most functional fastening for some items and can add decorative lacing to an otherwise plain area.

Choosing zips

It is most important not to use zips that are too heavy for the fabric. There are differing views on the merits of zips with metal teeth as opposed to plastic, so the choice really comes down to personal preference.

Setting in a zip

The instructions below describe the most widely used method of setting in a zip, which is suitable for most cushions, loose covers and clothes. It can be adapted easily to set in the zip centrally rather than to one side.

1 Lay the zip on the seam into which it will be set, so that the top end of the zip tape is in line with the top edge of the seam. Put in a pin immediately below the stopper at the bottom of the teeth.
2 Make the seam in the usual way, except sew only up to the pin marking the end of the zip, and backstitch firmly. Neaten the edges of the seam allowance for the whole length of the seam. Press the seam open, folding back the open part by exactly the same width and pressing this as well (fig 1).
3 With the zip closed, lay it right side up on a table. With the right side up, lay the left side (as you look at it) of the seam over the zip. Align the top edge of the seam with the top end of the zip tapes, lapping the folded edge over the teeth and slightly on to the tape on the right. Put in a pin parallel to the line of teeth and to hold the seam to the tape. Continue pinning below the first pin, heads down, so that the edge of the seam overlaps the teeth by the same amount (fig 2).
The pins mark the stitching line, so must not go in closer to the teeth than the machine zip foot is able to; you will need to experiment to determine this distance. (The zip foot will not allow the stitches to stay close to the teeth as it passes the zip pull. To remedy, open the zip a little, stitch, stop above pull, lift zip

foot, pull zip pull up, lower foot and stitch on: repeat in reverse at top of second side).
4 When you reach the end of the first side, put in a pin horizontally, exactly below the end of the stopper. This acts as a guide, so that you will know where to sew across the seam without hitting the zip end and breaking the needle.
5 Turn everything round so that the top of the zip is towards you. Working on the second side of the seam and starting at the lower end, butt the free edge up against the folded edge of the first side and put in a pin, again parallel to the zip teeth but this time very close to the seam edge. Continue pinning to the top. The pins on the second side should face in the opposite direction to those on the first side (fig 3).

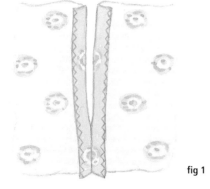

fig 1

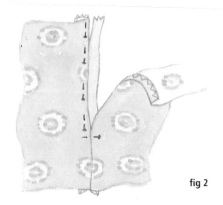

fig 2

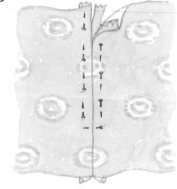

fig 3

6 Set your sewing machine to make a medium stitch and attach the zip foot, setting it so that it is open to the right. Starting with the first side, put the fabric into the machine so that the needle is exactly in line with the pins and about 5mm (¼in) below the top. Lower the foot and backstitch three or four stitches to the top. Then stitch forward from pin to pin, using them as a guide and removing each one as you come to it, right to the bottom of the zip. Leave the needle in the fabric.

7 Lift the foot and turn the fabric so that the foot faces across the end marked by the pin, which should now be removed. Lower the foot and stitch across the end, leaving the needle in the fabric.

8 Lift the foot again and turn the fabric so that the foot faces up the second side and along the line of pins. Lower the foot and stitch very close to the edge up to the top, removing each pin as you come to it. Finish with three or four backstitches.

Setting on a placket

1 Cut a piece of fabric the same length as the zip tapes and about 10cm (4in) wide. Fold it in half lengthways, right sides together, and stitch across one end. Turn right side out, folding as before. Press the fold and the stitched end. Pin and stitch the edges together.

2 On the side of the zip stitched close to the edge and from the wrong side, lay the placket over the seam allowance, with cut edges together and the neatened end at the bottom. Put your fingers under the seam allowance and pin the placket to the seam allowance only, fold the edge back and stitch the placket close to the edge with zigzag (fig 4). Press from the wrong side.

Setting a zip into a piped seam

1 First set the piping on to the side of the seam which will lap over the zip.

2 Make a narrow facing (see pages 34–35) and set it on over the piping before sewing up the seam. Then follow the steps above.

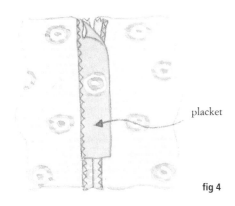

placket

fig 4

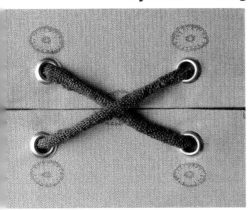

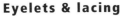

Eyelets & lacing

A simple way of fastening is to use eyelets with a cord threaded through them. It looks best if the fabric to be fastened exerts an even tension throughout, so that it does not gape open where the tension is weakest. The eyelets can be fixed into the fabric using a variety of methods, most often a specially adapted pair of pliers or a 'dolly', although these are specific to the eyelet kit they come with.

Eyelets are made in a variety of sizes, varying from the tiny ones used to lace up shoes to the large ones often employed on tents (see Garden Pavilion, page 42). Smaller eyelets can usually be purchased in haberdashery shops, but the larger ones are more difficult to find; canvas and camping gear shops sometimes sell them. The cushion shown on page 5 and in detail here, uses eyelets as a decorative fastening.

• Follow the instructions which come with your kit – there are no general instructions, as there are as many different methods of setting them in as there are brands of eyelet.

• Avoid fixing the eyelets too close to the edge, especially if the lacing will bear any weight as, for example, in a hammock.

• Always set the eyelets into a double layer of fabric and reinforce this with strong interfacing if necessary. Do bear in mind, however, that it is no use making the edge strong if the rest of the fabric is too weak to bear the weight it will have to carry.

• Any type of cord can be used for lacing, depending on its purpose. Where it is entirely decorative, a shiny twisted cord is attractive. A weight-bearing item will need a strong cord which does not stretch in any way.

49

buttonholes

Today, most sewing machines can make buttonholes semi-automatically. Follow the instructions in your sewing-machine handbook and, for best results, use the special foot if supplied. However, hand-stitched buttonholes are in a class of their own and it is well worth learning how to make them.

Hand-stitched buttonholes

Hand-stitched buttonholes are surprisingly quick and easy to make, and have the great advantage over machine-made ones that the thickness of the thread and the size of stitches can be adjusted to suit any fabric. Do practise on a scrap first.

Making a hand-stitched buttonhole

Hand-stitched buttonholes should be made on a double layer of fabric.

1 Lay the button on a tape measure to find the correct length for the buttonhole. If the button is unusually thick, make the buttonhole slightly longer; this can only be gauged by experience, so practise a few times to determine the correct length.

2 Mark this length on the fabric using tailor's chalk or a pencil; the outer end of the buttonhole should be on the centre line of the overlap. Cut along the line (through both layers) with small scissors, if possible making this cut run exactly between two threads (fig1).

3 Oversew (see page 27) all round to hold the two layers together (fig 2).

4 Work the buttonhole stitches: apart from the first stitch, all stitches are made by putting the needle into the right side of the fabric and bringing it out on the wrong side. Thread a needle with a long thread and make a knot in the end. Bring it through on to the right side, just below the inner end of the cut. Holding the thread back in a loop with your thumb, put the needle in immediately to the right of the first stitch and bring it up through the cut and then over the thread (fig 3).

5 Pull the thread through, forming a loop at the edge of the cut. Continue to hold the thread back with your thumb, put the needle in again immediately to the right of the last stitch and bring it up as before, needle over thread, forming another loop on the edge (fig 4). Continue to the end of the first side. The stitches should be an even length.

6 Fan out the stitches encircling the outer end and stitch the second side in the same way as the first (fig 5).

7 Finish the inner end of a buttonhole by making a row of buttonhole stitches at right angles to the others (see fig 5 and photograph above).

centre line

fig 1

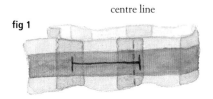

fig 2

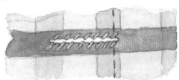

fig 3

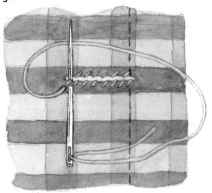

fig 4

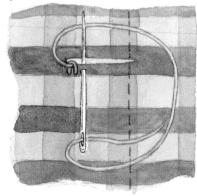

fig 5

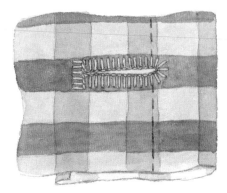

Bound buttonholes

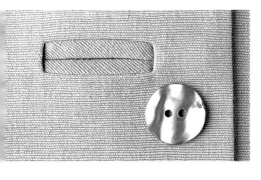

Bound buttonholes look very neat but do require some practice. They are easier to make with firm, closely woven but not stiff fabrics, which do not fray easily. If the main fabric does not fulfil these criteria, all is not lost: use one for the binding which does, perhaps in a contrasting colour or texture, thereby transforming the buttonhole into a decoration in its own right.

Making a bound buttonhole

1 Work out the length for the buttonhole and mark this on the right side of the fabric, as for hand-stitched buttonholes, but do not cut (fig 6).

2 Cut a bias strip the length of the buttonhole plus 4cm (1½in), and 6–7cm (2¼–3in) wide – the exact measurement depends on the size of the buttonhole and the thickness of the fabric, but it is better to err on the large side and trim it back at the end.

3 Mark the length of the buttonhole centrally on the wrong side of the bias strip. Mark a rectangle about 1cm (⅜in) wide around it; again, the exact measurement depends on the fabric. With right sides together, lay this accurately on the original mark and pin in place (fig 7).

4 Machine stitch all round the rectangle, using a slightly smaller stitch than usual. Staystitch the ends and corners over the original stitches.

5 Cut through the centre and right into the corners, (fig 8).

6 From the wrong side, pull the bias strip through the cut and fold both edges back to one side, pulling the top one back to prevent the strip rolling over the seam on the right side, and press the seam allowance over the strip (fig 9). Do the same on the second side. Then wrap and press the bias strip back, tightly, over the cut edge on each side, forming tiny pleats at the ends. Hold with a stitch at each end (fig 10).

7 From the right side, pin and tack each side in place so that the wrapped edges meet, pulling the tiny triangles (under the pleats on the wrong side) back to make the seams at the ends roll under, so that the ends are neat (fig 10).

Then either:

8 Machine stitch (use a zip foot if working with thicker fabrics) from the right side and close up against the original seam (fig 11).

Or:

8 Stitch by hand, from the wrong side, so that everything is held securely in place. Trim back any surplus fabric.

fig 6

centre line

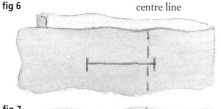

fig 7

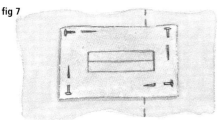

fig 8

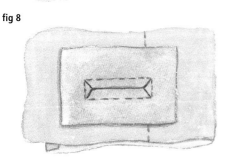

fig 9

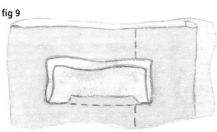

fig 10

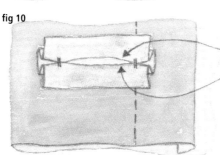

fig 11

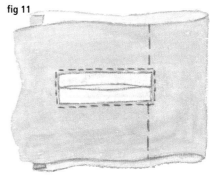

bring edges together to form pleats

buttons

Buttons are produced in an enormous range of materials, ranging from wood and metal to glass, stone, leather, mother-of-pearl and, of course, plastic. Many are decorative enough to form the sole ornament on a piece of work. For the perfect match, covered buttons or Chinese knots can be made from the same fabric as the rest of the article. Dorset or fringed buttons can be any colour or texture as they are made from embroidery threads. Decorative buttons should be removed before washing.

Covered buttons

Well-designed kits for covering buttons are widely available, making this an easy task. Almost any fabric can be used provided it is not too thick. If the fabric is transparent or very thin, use a double layer or a thicker one underneath; in this case, it is easiest to attach the two layers separately. It is sometimes difficult to get the fabric to catch on the little hooks, but this can usually be put right by dampening it. Fix two opposite sides, then the two sides at right angles to those and catch them evenly in-between.

Making a covered button
1 Cut out a circle of fabric to the correct size for the button you are making (this will be shown in the instructions that come with the kit).
2 Lay the button centrally on the wrong side of the circle (fig 1).
3 Stretch the fabric tightly over the button and catch it evenly all round on the hooks (fig 2).
4 Put the back plate in place and snap on using finger pressure like a press stud (fig 3).

fig 2

hooks

fig 1

fig 3

Fringed buttons

This attractive embellishment is simple to make and can be added to a plain button and used on a cushion, tie-back or anywhere else that needs extra decoration.

Making a fringed button
1 Thread a needle with doubled sewing thread and knot the end. Put several lengths of different embroidery threads together, each about 30cm (12in) long, and wind them around a pencil six or seven times. Push the loops up closely together and, holding the ends tightly, thread the sewing thread under and around them two or three times (fig 4).
2 Slide the threads off the pencil, pull up tightly and knot underneath (fig 5).
3 Use the remaining thread to sew on the button in the usual way. Cut through the loops, fluff them up and trim the ends evenly. Experiment with thinner or thicker pencils to make the fringe exactly the right size.

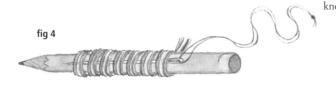

knot

fig 4

fig 5

Dorset buttons

There are as many designs for Dorset buttons as there are people making them. Once the basic method has been mastered, it is easy and fun to work out different stitches and patterns. One of the simplest to make is known as the Dorset Crosswheel, so this is a good one to start with.

Making a Dorset button
You will need

• A ring the size of the finished button. This can be made of brass, steel or plastic, and the thinner it is the finer will be the result. Curtain rings come in a suitable range of sizes, are usually washable and will not rust, so these are ideal. Start with a 2.5cm (1in) ring.
• Thread. Most types can be used, but the easiest is a well-twisted, smooth embroidery thread, such as pearl cotton. Stranded embroidery cotton tends to knot, so avoid this at first.
• A tapestry needle of the correct size for the thread.

To make up

1 Thread the needle with a thread about 2.5m (3yd) long (for a 2.5cm/1in ring) and make a knot over the ring (fig 6).
2 Make four or five buttonhole stitches around the ring and over the short end of thread (fig 7). Cut this end off against the last stitch.
3 Continue making buttonhole stitches close together all round the ring.
4 Join the stitches by passing the needle through the knot on the first stitch and pulling the thread tight (fig 8).
5 Roll the stitches over so that the knots are on the inside of the ring (fig 9).
6 Wind the thread tightly round the ring to make twelve spokes, spaced out evenly like the hours on a clock (figs 9 and 10). **NB** Each spoke consists of two strands of thread, one on the back and one on the front: only the latter are shown in fig 10.
7 Bring the needle through from back to front in the centre, take it over to the opposite side of the crossed spokes, still in the centre, and stitch through to the wrong side. Make several more stitches, pulling them tight and thus binding the spokes together in the centre, forming a little boss (fig 11). It is important to keep these binding stitches, and therefore the crossing point, exactly in the centre, or the button will end up looking lopsided.
8 From the back, bring the thread up on to the right side at the centre between two spokes. Make a backstitch over one spoke and under two. Continue making backstitches in this way, pulling the thread firmly and keeping the tension even (fig 11). Stitch round and round until you reach the ring edge.
9 Weave the thread through the back to the centre and finish off by stitching into the central boss.

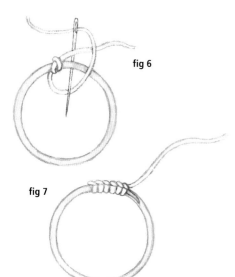

fig 6

fig 7

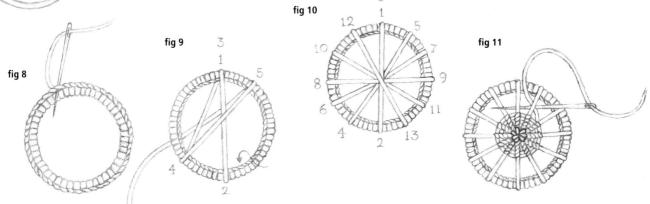

fig 8

fig 9

fig 10

fig 11

53

Chinese knot buttons

These are the buttons used so widely on clothes and bags made in China. They are particularly useful on pyjamas or nightdresses, as they are soft and comfortable to lie on but are very decorative too. Although it takes a while to learn the knack, Chinese knots are quicker and easier to make than they look and, like bicycling, once learnt never forgotten. As they will receive lots of wear, choose a firm, closely woven fabric, avoiding those that are too thick or are likely to fray easily; otherwise, experiment with anything you fancy and have fun making these natty little knots.

Making a Chinese knot
Piping cord is the easiest material with which to practise.
1 Cut a piece of cord 75cm (30in) long. Roll adhesive tape tightly around the ends to prevent them unravelling.
2 Lay the cord centrally over your left hand (fig 1).
3 Bring the end of the cord from the back up to the front and form a loop on your palm (fig 2).
4 Using your thumb, hold the crossing point of this loop against the middle finger of your left hand. Curl the front end of the cord round to the right, under the back end, then up and curl it round to the left, threading it through the loop as shown (fig 3).
5 Curl the front end down and round to the right, under two and over two as shown. Curl the back end up and round to the left, under two and over two as shown (fig 4).
6 Slide the whole thing off your hand and turn it over carefully, keeping all the strands in place. Put it back on your left hand, upside down, allowing the two ends to hang down between your index and middle fingers. Gradually ease each of the loops round, taking the excess down between your fingers and thus tightening them (fig 5). This needs perseverance, but it will eventually form a small, tight ball.

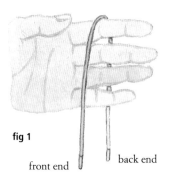

fig 1

front end   back end

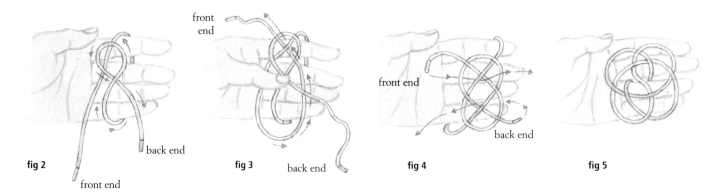

front
end

fig 2

front end   back end

fig 3   back end

front end   back end

fig 4

fig 5

When you have mastered the technique of making Chinese knots with piping cord, make one using a rouleau strip. To make the strip:
1 Cut a bias strip (see page 21) about 75cm (30in) long and 2.5cm (1in) wide.
2 With right sides together, fold in half lengthways and stitch about 4–6mm (⅛–¼in) from the fold.
3 Turn through using a blunt needle.

Setting on the button
1 Cut the long ends off the knotted button to the required length plus turning. Use one of these ends to form the buttonhole loop.
2 Lay in position opposite each other. Turn in the ends to neaten.
3 Tack in place and check that the loop fits snugly over the knot. Stitch firmly and neatly in place by hand.

ties & straps

Besides their obvious functions, ties and straps can add decoration if made from contrasting colours and textures. Make them from fabric or such materials as cord, ribbon, rope, braid or leather. The occasional chain can even be utilized. Always consider the purpose for which they will be used and choose something that can contend with this type of wear. Fabric ties and straps can both be made in various different ways, two of which are given below, and they can both be reinforced with interlining if necessary. Use a strong thread to stitch ties which will take plenty of wear.

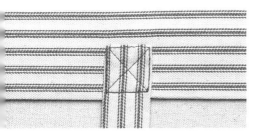

Making fabric ties

1 Cut a strip of fabric to the required length for the ties and twice the finished width, adding a seam allowance all round.
2 With right sides together, fold in half lengthways and stitch across one end and down the side.

3 Turn right side out, using a safety pin or blunt knitting needle to push the stitched end through the tube of fabric to the other, open, end.
4 Press the tie, turning in the open end neatly. Pin in place and stitch a rectangle to secure it. See below for another way to make ties and set them in.

ticking bag

This simple bag with a useful zipped pocket can be made from a strong cotton or linen fabric such as ticking, canvas or sailcloth.

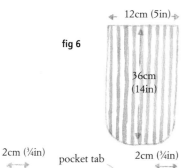

← 12cm (5in) →

fig 6

36cm (14in)

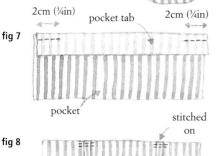

2cm (¾in)   2cm (¾in)
pocket tab

fig 7

pocket

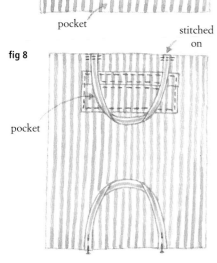

fig 8

pocket

stitched on

pocket

You will need

120cm (48in) fabric, 110cm (44in) wide
20cm (8in) zip
Matching sewing thread

To cut out

2 main pieces, 76 (along the stripe) x 45cm (30 x 18in)
4 gussets, 36 (along the stripe) x 15cm (14 x 6in). Fold in half lengthways and round off one end (fig 6)
2 straps, 85 (along the stripe) x 10cm (33 x 4in)
1 pocket piece, 18 x 24cm (7 x 9½in)
1 pocket tab, 8 x 24cm (3 x 9½in)

To make up

Use 2cm (¾in) seam allowances throughout.
1 With right sides together, lay one pocket piece on the other, matching long edges, and pin. Stitch seams for 2cm (¾in) at each end, and backstitch firmly at the ends to strengthen them (fig 7). Press the seam open and set in the zip (see page 48).
2 Press 2cm (¾in) to the wrong side all round the pocket. Lay it centrally about 10cm (4in) below the shorter edge of one of the main pieces. Pin and stitch close to the edge, 1cm (⅜in) in.
3 On both long sides of each strap, press 1cm (⅜in) over on to the wrong side. Press over again so that the edges meet in the middle. Stitch close to each edge. Lay the straps on a main piece, right sides together, with the ends on a short side and about 12cm (5in) apart. Pin and stitch across the ends (fig 8).
4 With right sides together, lay the long side of a gusset on the long side of a main piece, matching at the top. Pin down one side, round the curved end of the gusset and up the other side, and stitch. Set on the second gusset in the same way, and the remaining two on to the second main piece as a lining.
5 With right sides together, push one main piece inside the other, pin all round the top edge and stitch. Unpick 10cm (4in) on one of the gusset seams and turn the bag right side out through it. Push the main piece with the pocket on it inside the other one and press the top edge. Pull the straps away and topstitch all round the top, 1cm (⅜in) from the edge. Oversew the opening in the gusset seam.

beach cushions

Made from hardwearing but decorative fabrics, these two simple cushions are trimmed either with contrasting ties or with a reversed band of the same fabric. Strong cotton ticking, canvas, calico or sailcloth would all be suitable. Wash the fabric first as some calico and sailcloths are prone to shrinking.

Tied cushion

fig 1

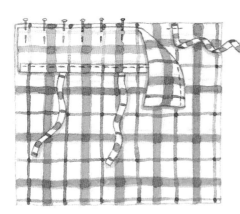

You will need

Enough fabric for:
2 x 70cm (28in) squares
   70 x 20cm (28in x 8 in) strip for flap
In a contrasting fabric, 6 strips for ties: 35cm x 9cm (14 x 3½in)
Matching sewing thread
70cm (28in) square cushion pad

To make up

1 Fold each tie strip in half lengthways, right sides together, and sew the long edges and one end. Turn and press.
2 Make a double hem along one long edge of the flap.

3 Position three ties evenly along one edge of a square, with open ends on the edge, lay the flap right side down on top (fig 1), matching the edges, pin and stitch. Trim seam allowances, fold the flap to the wrong inside and press.
4 Make a double hem on one side of the second square, then lay right sides together over the first square with the finished edges together. Pin and stitch the remaining sides.
5 Turn the cover right side out and lay the remaining three ties inside the free edge in line with the front ties, fold raw ends under and stitch securely.

Buttoned cushion

You will need

Enough fabric for:
main piece 70 x 105cm (28 x 42in), with stripes parallel to shorter side.
band 28 x 105cm (11 x 42in), with stripes running along its length
Matching sewing thread
2 buttons
70cm (28in) square cushion pad

To make up

1 Fold the band in half lengthways, wrong sides together, and press. Press 2cm (¾in) on to the wrong side along one long edge. Neaten half its length with zigzag. Stitch down the neatened part 1.5cm (⅝in) from the edge.
2 Lay the free long edge of the band on one long edge of the main piece, right sides together, matching ends and edges. Pin and stitch with a 2cm (¾in) seam allowance and press this over the band. Neaten edges of half the seam to match the stitching on the outer edge.
3 Fold the band and main piece in half, right sides together (fig 2), bringing the short ends of the band together and

matching the edges all round the cover. Refold the ends of the band in half to lie on the seam, then pin across the ends, down the side and across the lower edge (fig 3). Stitch and turn right side out.
4 Pin the unzigzagged edge of the band to the wrong side of the seam and topstitch in place. Make two buttonholes through both layers of fabric on this side of the band and mark the position for the buttons through them on to the loose inner flap. Pin small squares of fabric on the wrong side of the marks and zigzag all round to strengthen. Sew buttons on marks.

fig 2

fig 3

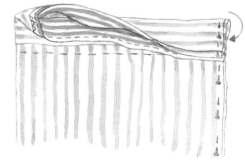

rabbit-eared cushion

This whimsical cushion exploits the different textures and tones of undyed natural fabrics. Calico, linen or even hessian would all provide suitable neutral shades, but a similar effect could be achieved using a range of subtle colours. The fish are added as appliqué shapes caught under a muslin patch. It would be easy to exchange the fish motif for other simple shapes such as: stars, trees, rabbits or even geometrical pieces, which would give the cushion your own individual stamp.

fig 1

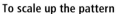

fig 2

3cm (1in) seam allowance

clip

trim points

fig 3

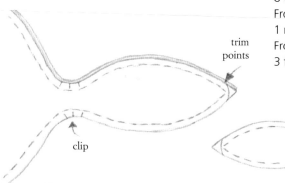

3cm (1in) gap

trim points

fig 4

You will need

Piece calico or other natural cotton, linen or similar fabric, 170 x 90cm (66 x 36in)
Piece muslin or other transparent fabric, 36 x 8cm (14 x 3in)
3 pieces white or pale-coloured fabric, 8 x 12cm (3 x 5in), for the fish
Beads, for fish eyes and corners
Matching sewing and embroidery threads
30cm (12in) zip
55cm (22in) square cushion pad

To scale up the pattern

Following the pattern diagram on page 105, fold an 80cm (32in) square of paper accurately in half and then in half again, then draw on the main piece and tie. The fish is shown full size.

To cut out

From calico:
1 main piece
2 pieces, using the pattern for the main piece cut in half (through one of the folds) + 3cm (1in) seam allowance added to each side of the cut edges
8 tie pieces
From muslin:
1 rectangle, 36 x 8cm (14 x 3in)
From white or pale-coloured fabric:
3 fish

To make up

1 Pin the fish in place on the main fabric piece, checking that the muslin patch fits over them, and then hand stitch in place lightly using sewing thread.
2 Pin the muslin patch in place and machine stitch all round about 1cm (⅜in) inside the edge, using a small stitch. One by one, gently pull threads away from each side of the muslin to make a fringe.
3 Using embroidery thread, make small running stitches around each of the fish and sew on beads for the eyes.
4 Lay the zip centrally on the straight edge of one of the half pieces and make a notch at each end of the teeth (fig 1). Lay the half pieces right sides together, with the straight edges matching, and pin. Using a 3cm (1in) seam allowance, stitch from each end up to each notch and backstitch (fig 2). Press the seam open. Set the zip into the seam as described on page 48.
5 Open the zip and then pin the two main pieces right sides together all round the edge. Stitch all round using a 1.5cm (⅝in) seam allowance, reducing to 7mm (¼in) around the 'ears'. Staystitch around the ears, using a smaller stitch. Trim the points and clip into the seam allowance on the curves (fig 3). Turn right side out and press.
6 With right sides together, pin four pairs of tie pieces all round the edge and stitch round with a 5mm (¼in) seam allowance, leaving a 3cm (1in) gap in the centre (fig 4). Staystitch, trim and clip the seam as before. Turn each tie right side out through the gap and close it with slipstitch. Press. Sew beads on each corner and knot the ties on to each corner of the cushion.

waistcoat with Chinese knots

This classic waistcoat is quite easy to sew and can be made up in a wide variety of fabrics, from cool summery linens to warm winter woollens, making it an ideal gift for any occasion. The Chinese knot buttons (see page 54) require some practice, but provide an unusual finish to the waistcoat and will certainly impress your friends! Spend some time learning the knack and you will be surprised at how quick they are to make and how many places you can find to use them.

A striped brocade was used for the waistcoat illustrated and the front has been interlined with medium-weight cotton to give it extra body; for a softer look, a very light interfacing could be substituted. For a large area such as this it is better not to use an iron-on interfacing, as this sometimes bubbles or comes away when washed.

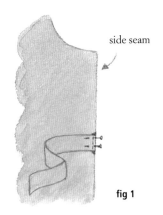

side seam

fig 1

You will need
90cm (1yd) main fabric, 120cm (48in) wide
140cm (1½yd) lining fabric, 120cm (48in) wide
90cm (1yd) interlining, 110cm (42in) wide
Matching sewing thread
Waistcoat buckle

NB If the waistcoat is to be washed, wash all three fabrics first to shrink them, as each fabric may have a different rate of shrinkage.

To scale up the pattern
Scale up the pattern from the diagram on page 102. Remember to mark all the notches, straight grain lines and the placement lines for the belt.

To cut out
From main fabric:
1 pair fronts
    1 placket
    3 bias-cut strips, 3.5 x 50cm (1½ x 20in), for the Chinese knots
    3 bias-cut strips, 3.5 x 30cm (1½ x 12in), for the loops
From lining fabric:
2 backs, one to line the other
    1 pair fronts, to line fronts
    2 pieces 30 x 7cm (12 x 3in), for belt
    1 placket
From interlining fabric:
1 pair fronts
    1 placket

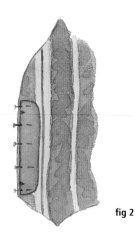

fig 2

To make up
NB Because the waistcoat is fully lined, there is no need to neaten the edges of any of the seams, just trim away any bulky material.

1 Fold the belt strips in half lengthways, right sides together, then pin and stitch across one end and down the side. Turn right side out using a safety pin or blunt knitting needle and press. Lay the strips on the right side of one of the backs (fig 1), open ends between the notches on the side seams, pin and stitch in place. This will now be the main back.

2 Pin the interlining in place on the wrong side of the fronts and stitch all round close to the edge, using a large machine stitch.

3 Lay the fronts on the main back, right sides together, matching at the shoulder seams. Pin and stitch. Press the seam allowances under the back and topstitch on the back, close to the seam.

4 Make the shoulder seams on the lining in the same way, but press the seams open and do not topstitch.

5 Pin the interlining on the wrong side of the placket and stitch all round, close to the edge. Pin the lining on the placket, right sides together. Stitch round three sides, leaving the notched side open. Turn right side out and press. Topstitch 5mm (¼in) from the seam. Pin the notched edges together and stitch close to the edge.

6 Lay the placket on the left waistcoat front (fig 2), right sides together and matching the notches. Pin and stitch close to the edge.

7 Lay the waistcoat on the lining (fig 3), right sides together. Pin the neck edges together at the centre back and continue all round, matching up the neck ends of the shoulder seams, the notches on the front edges, the points on the lower edge and the ends of the side seams.

8 Pin the armholes from the side seam up to the shoulder seam and back to the other side seam, matching the front and back notches as you go. Pin the lower edges of the back together.

9 Stitch from the side seam across the lower edge of the front, turning on the needle at the point. Continue up the front, across the end of the shoulder seam, around the back neck and back down the second side in the same way as the first.

10 Make staystitches around the points and trim the fabric back close to them. Clip into the seam allowance wherever necessary to allow it to lie flat when it is turned the right way out.

11 Stitch the armholes from the side seam round to the shoulder seam and down to the side seam at the other end. Clip the seam allowance as before.

12 Stitch across the lower edge of the back, turning on the needle to form a sharp angle at each of the three central points. Staystitch around all three points, clip in to the central one and trim back to the stitches on the two lower points (fig 4).

13 Turn the waistcoat right side out by pushing your hand up between the two layers of each back side seam and pulling each of the fronts through. Press all the stitched edges, rolling the seams to lie on the inside.

14 Pin the two layers of the back side seams together and stitch close to the edge. Lay the main front side seam on the back side seam, right sides together, keeping the front lining and seam allowances at each end free. Stitch and press so that the seam allowance lies under the front.

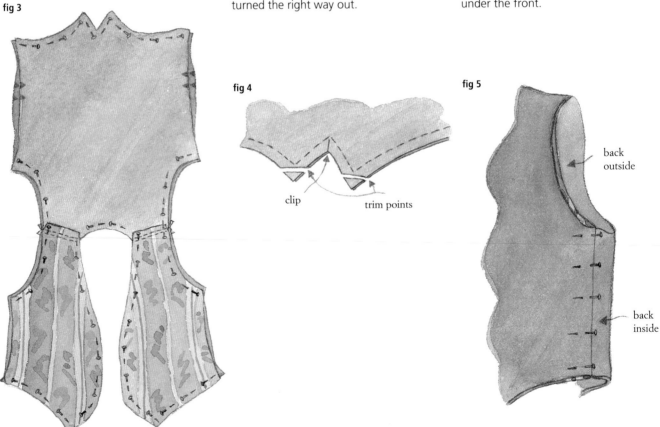

fig 3

fig 4

clip   trim points

fig 5

back outside

back inside

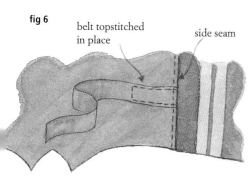

fig 6

belt topstitched in place

side seam

15 Press the seam allowance on the front lining to the wrong side and lap this over the seam allowance, close up against the stitches on the side seam (fig 5). Pin at right angles to the seam, turn to the right side, and topstitch on the front close to the seam. Press.

16 Pin the belt ends in place on the waistcoat back (see placement lines on the pattern) through both layers of the back. Stitch along both sides and across the end (fig 6). Loop the buckle over one end of the belt and stitch in place, using a zip foot if necessary to get the stitches close enough to the buckle.

17 Press the whole waistcoat very carefully, then neatly topstitch around all the edges.

18 Make the Chinese buttons and matching loops as described on page 54, using the longer strips of fabric to make the knots and shorter ones for the loops. Mark their positions on the front edges and stitch in place.

63

bean bag

Make bean bags for comfortable informal seating inside or out. They are ideal for a child's bedroom or playroom. Choose a tough, washable furnishing fabric for the cover. As the polystyrene beans are a potential choking hazard to young children, it is essential to make a strong lining, with topstitched seams and opening, to hold the beans securely.

You will need

2.3m (2½yd) strong fabric, 120cm (48in) wide
2.3m (2½yd) calico, 120cm (48in) wide
120cm (48in) zip
Strong sewing thread
Polystyrene beans

To draw the pattern and cut out

1 Draw up the pattern pieces for side panels, base and top (figs 1,2,3 and pattern diagram on page 104).
2 Cut out six side panels, one base and one top from both fabrics.

To make up

Use 2cm (¾in) seam allowances throughout.
1 On both cover and lining, lay one side panel on another, right sides together. Pin along one long edge and stitch, backstitching at each end. Open out and join the other four side pieces in the same way, but do not make the final seams on either cover or lining.
2 Press all the seam allowances to one side and topstitch 1cm (⅜in) from the seam. Bring the remaining side panels right sides together, and make and

topstitch the final seams on the cover and lining in the same way.
3 On the cover, press the seam allowance on five sides of the base on to the wrong side and lap this over the zip teeth. Pin and stitch.
4 With right sides together, lay the base at the wider (base) end of the side panels. Match the edges of the zip to the edge of five of the sides and the free edge of the base to the sixth side panel, pin and stitch. Press the seam allowance to lie under the sides and topstitch.
5 On the lining, stitch the sides on to the base in a similar way, leaving one side open and topstitch as for the cover.
6 Open the zip. On both cover and lining, and with right sides together, lay the top on the top end of the side panels, matching all six sides. Pin and stitch all round. Turn both pieces right side out and topstitch.
7 Place the lining inside the cover and fill it half to three-quarters full with polystyrene beans (make a funnel for the beans with a rolled newspaper). Pinch the open edges of the lining together, pin and machine with two rows of stitching. Close the zip.

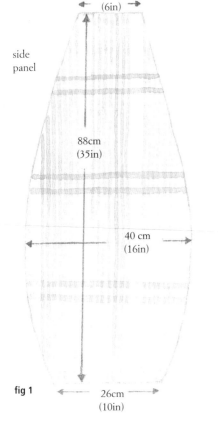

15cm
(6in)

side
panel

88cm
(35in)

40 cm
(16in)

fig 1

26cm
(10in)

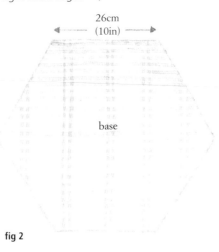

26cm
(10in)

base

fig 2

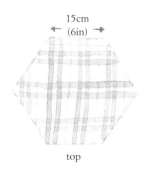

15cm
(6in)

top

fig 3

drawstring bag

The instructions given here can be used for making bags of any size, from tiny ones in which to store small pieces of jewellery up to large ones big enough to hold the washing. They are ideal for using up remnants and can be embellished with an embroidered panel, as shown here. Once you have made one drawstring bag using these instructions, it is easy to adapt them to make many other types of bag.

You will need

Fabric remnants for bag, embroidered panel, channel and tie
Length of decorative edging, same length as top of bag
Matching sewing thread

To draw the pattern and cut out

1 Using tailor's chalk, draw out a rectangle on the wrong side of the fabric to the finished size of the bag. Draw another the same size to make the second side of the bag, either on one side (fig 1) or on the end (fig 2), *or* draw one rectangle on a double layer of fabric (fig 3), whichever fits best.

2 Add the width required for the frill to the top on all three versions.

3 Add seam allowances all round and cut out.

4 Cut a rectangle for the embroidered panel from contrasting fabric, to the required size plus seam allowances.

5 Cut a strip for the channel in contrasting fabric, twice the length of the finished width of the bag x twice the finished width of the drawstring plus seam allowances on all sides.

6 Cut a strip for the drawstring about 20cm (8in) longer than the channel strip x twice the finished width required plus seam allowances on all sides.

To make up

1 Embroider the panel. Press the seam allowances to the wrong side, then lay the panel on the bag, pin and topstitch.

2 For a bag made from two pieces, lay these right sides together, then pin and stitch the sides and lower edge. For a bag made from one piece, fold in half, pin and stitch the lower edge or sides.

3 Neaten the top edge of the bag. Turn a narrow double turning onto the wrong side and stitch close to the inner edge. Pin the edging round the top on the wrong side and stitch in place.

4 Press all seam allowances on the channel to the wrong side and stitch across each end. Lay it on the right side of the bag, right side up and along the frill line. Pin and topstitch along both edges. (On small bags, stitch on the channel before stitching the side seam).

5 Fold the drawstring fabric in half lengthways, with right sides together. Stitch across one end and along the side to the centre, leave a gap and then stitch up to and across the other end. Turn each end right side out through the gap using a blunt knitting needle. Slipstitch the gap.

6 Thread the drawstring into the channel using a safety pin. Knot the drawstring ends together.

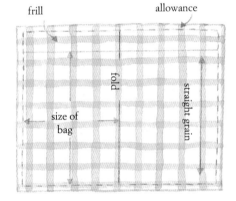

frill | seam allowance

size of bag | fold | straight grain

fig 1

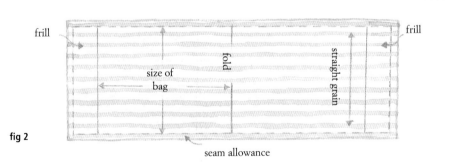

frill | frill

size of bag | fold | straight grain

seam allowance

fig 2

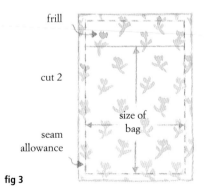

frill

cut 2

size of bag

seam allowance

fig 3

Trimmings & decoration

Most people like decoration, and whatever they make, they decorate. This is as true for clothing and household articles as it is for architecture. With sufficient imagination and experience, it is possible to adapt the techniques from the previous chapters to form trimmings and decorations. Luckily, however, there are also easier options: sewing techniques which are innately decorative and not too difficult for the comparative newcomer to sewing to use imaginatively to enhance their work. A selection of these techniques – frilling and fringing, piping and pintucking, chevrons and scallops – are described in this chapter, ready to entice you into the pleasure to be found in decorative sewing. They are the icing on the cake: without purpose, but full of delight.

gathers, frills & rosettes

Gathering is sometimes referred to as 'drawing up', which also describes how 'gathers' are made. 'Gauging' – an old-fashioned word for gathering – is still used on paper patterns to indicate the minimal and almost invisible gathers used to form a softly rounded shape, most often on sleeve heads. Gathering can be done by hand but is obviously much quicker by machine, especially if a lot of fabric is to be gathered.

Frills are strips of fabric of varying widths that are gathered along one edge. They are usually cut on the straight grain, but can be cut on the cross to give a different, usually softer effect. Frills look particularly luxurious if this effect is combined with folding them in half lengthways. Rosettes are exuberant trimmings which are very easy to make from gathered fabric or ribbon.

Making gathers

By machine

Adjust the machine to make the longest possible stitch. Some machines will also need the tension loosened to allow the threads to be drawn up (refer to your sewing-machine handbook). Check the gathering stitch on a fabric scrap to see that it gathers easily.

1 Make a row of stitches close to the edge to be gathered. Make a second row of stitches, close to and just above the first stitching line and, ideally, a third row just below the stitching line (fig 1).

2 On small pieces, backstitch firmly at one end; on large pieces, leave both ends free. Leave a good length of thread at the free end(s).

3 Draw up the bobbin threads (on the underside of the fabric) only, from one end on small pieces and both ends on large ones. Do this gently, a little at a time and drawing up all three rows of thread together, to approximately the required length (fig 2).

By hand

Use a double thread, a bit longer than the edge to be gathered.

1 Make three rows of small running stitches (of the same length on both sides of the fabric) as before, using a separate double thread for each row.

2 Try to line up the stitches, as this helps the gathers to lie in nice little 'pipes' – this is the only advantage hand-sewn gathers have over machine-sewn ones. On small pieces, fasten off the end at the beginning only; on larger ones, leave both ends free.

3 Draw up the three threads carefully to approximately the length required for the gathered section.

For both methods

4 Put in a pin at right angles to the gathering line at the end(s) and use it as a cleat to hold the thread. Trim off some of the surplus thread (fig 3).

5 Even out the gathers by gentle easing.

fig 1

backstitch at beginning

fig 2

fig 3

pin used as cleat

Setting on gathers

1 With right sides together, lay the flat piece of fabric on top of the gathered piece, matching ends and edges. Pin at right angles to the edge, adjusting and rearranging the gathers to fit.
2 Stroke down hand-stitched gathers with a blunt needle to form neat pipes.
3 Unwind the thread from the pin(s) and knot off firmly.
4 With the flat piece on top, stitch the seam using the normal stitch size for the fabric. Trim away any bulky seam allowance and press the seam allowance to lie under the flat side.
5 Unpick the third row of gathering.

Helpful hints

● To work out how much fabric is required, gather up a measured piece of the fabric until it looks as full as required, measure it again and use this to work out the amount needed.
● It is sometimes necessary to mark centres and quarters to help keep the gathers even. Use a hand stitch in a contrasting colour, as notches tend to get lost among the gathers.
● Sometimes when setting on gathers, the flat piece of fabric draws up slightly. To rectify this, 'tension' the fabric as you sew the seam (see page 27).

Making frills

Frills are drawn up in exactly the same way as gathers. The length to cut the frill can only be worked out by experimenting: it varies from adding half as much again to three or even four times as much, depending on the fabric and the effect required. If you are making a large item with frills, do not underestimate the amount of extra fabric you will need to buy for the frills.

There are several methods for finishing the edges:
● Turn over by 2–3mm (⅛in) and stitch close to the edge. Trim this close to the stitching, turn the edge over again and stitch. This is usually referred to as 'neatening the edge twice', and the narrower it is the better it looks.
● On thicker fabrics, neaten the edge with zigzag, turn over again and stitch close to the free edge.
● Cut thin fabrics to double the required width and fold in half. The two edges are then gathered as one.
● Cut fabrics which do not fray readily with pinking shears.
● Finish the raw edge with zigzag set close enough to prevent it fraying.

Making rosettes

● Rosettes can be made from circles of fabric gathered tightly around the edge (fig 4), with covered buttons used to conceal the stitches in the middle.
● Hem a strip and gather along the opposite edge to form a circle (fig 5).
● Use folded bias strips, trimmed to a point at one end, and drawn up through the cut edges to form a spiral (fig 6).
● Ribbon can also be gathered up to form pretty rosettes.

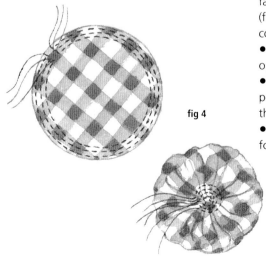

fig 4

fold

bias strip for spiral rosette

fig 6

forming a spiral rosette

smaller contrasting rosette in centre

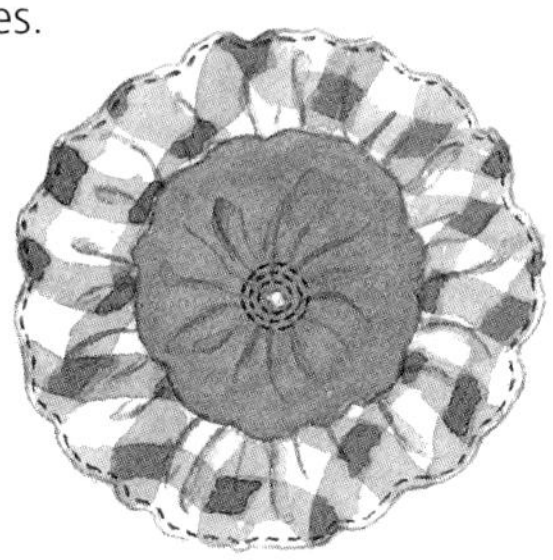

fig 5

stitched hem

pintucks

These tiny tucks have no purpose other than the purely decorative, but at this they excel. One or two have little value, five or six will add both texture and pattern.

The name itself suggests that these tucks are as narrow as a pin, and this is true when they are made on fabrics such as lawn and fine cottons. Made on heavier fabrics, they will be much fatter and fewer will be needed to make an impression.

Making pintucks

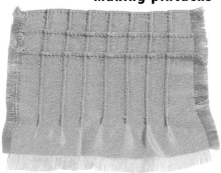

fig 1

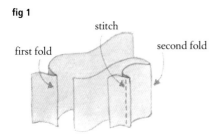

first fold   stitch   second fold

fig 2

stitch

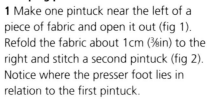

fig 3   unpressed pintucks right side

fig 4   unpressed pintucks wrong side

1 To practise, fold a small piece of fabric, right side out, on the straight grain and stitch close to the edge. Make several more pintucks parallel to the first, but with different distances between them.

2 Choose the width of tuck that suits the fabric: too wide, and they will look clumsy; too narrow, and they will just form a ridge, not a tuck. Practise until you can sew the pintucks evenly.

Grouping pintucks

1 Make one pintuck near the left of a piece of fabric and open it out (fig 1). Refold the fabric about 1cm (⅜in) to the right and stitch a second pintuck (fig 2). Notice where the presser foot lies in relation to the first pintuck.

2 Open out and refold again, using your eyes and the foot as guides to keep the width between the tucks the same, and stitch a third tuck (figs 3 and 4). Continue in this way until you have made the required number of pintucks.

3 Press the tucks to one side from the wrong side using the point of the iron.

Helpful hints

- Do not press the pintucks before stitching them – this makes the job more difficult, not less.
- Form pintucks on fabric before cutting out pattern pieces.
- Work from left to right: this prevents wodges of fabric getting stuck under the machine.
- Avoid stitching up one pintuck and down the next, as this tends to distort the fabric. Start all the tucks from the same end.
- Do not use too small a stitch, as this will tend to stiffen the seam. Use the same thread as for the rest of the article, and do not use thread that is too thick as this will make the stitches look clumsy and show up too much.

Making crossed pintucks

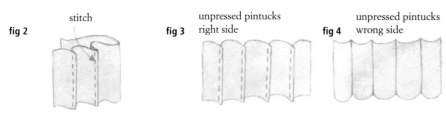

press first group

fig 5

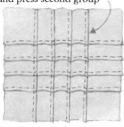

stitch and press second group

fig 6

1 Work out where you want to begin your group of pintucks and mark the first one on the edge of the fabric.

2 Stitch the first group of parallel pintucks and press them thoroughly, ensuring that they all lie in one direction (fig 5).

3 Fold the fabric at right angles to the first group to form the crossed pintucks. Stitch each pintuck slowly, taking great care that the original tucks are not twisted as the machine goes over them. Use the point of a pair of scissors to hold them if they are twisting; some machines catch more than others.

4 Fold the fabric for a second tuck, stitch and repeat to finish the required number. Press to one side (fig 6).

pleats

A pleat consists of a visible outer fold of fabric and a concealed inner fold. An unpressed pleat is made by folding a piece of fabric at the top only and taking this fold over to one side, whereas a pressed pleat is folded at top and bottom and creased along the length. Box pleats and inverted pleats are made by folding pleats to face in opposite directions, a row of box pleats will have inverted pleats behind them and inverted pleats will have box pleats behind them (see below). Most fabrics can be made into unpressed pleats, but pressed pleats require a fabric which will take and hold a sharp crease.

Making pleats

1 Decide how wide to make each pleat, and work out how many will be needed. The inner fold is usually made twice as wide as the outer, although this depends on how much fullness is required (fig 7).

2 Clip notches at the top of the fabric to mark the top folds and pleat lines (fig 8). For pressed pleats, make the hem and then use pins on it to correspond with the notches at the top (fig 9).

3 For unpressed pleats, fold through the notches at the top to form the pleats, pin and stitch close to the edge.

4 For pressed pleats, make the first top fold using the notches as a guide, pin at both ends, pull apart to straighten and press from end to end. Press all the top folds in the same way. Take the top folds over to lie on the pleat lines, forming the pleat, and pin at both ends. Press as before and stitch across the top.

fig 7

pleats with different amounts folded in

fig 8

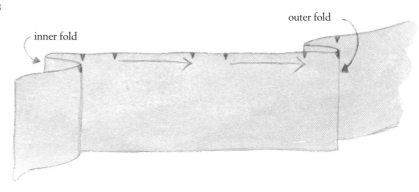

inner fold

outer fold

fig 9   pressed pleats

add seam allowance

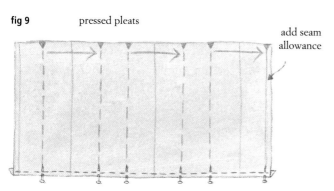

box and inverted pleats

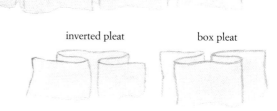

inverted pleat   box pleat

frilled pillowcase

Decorative bedlinen is expensive to buy and it is often difficult to find exactly what you like. Pillowcases and duvet covers are quick, easy and comparatively cheap to make. This pillowcase requires just a few seams and a little gathering.

Use cotton sheeting or a similar lightweight fabric for this project – if you choose checks, make sure that they are woven or printed at right angles to the selvedge, and that the lines of the checks are straight.

You will need

Cotton sheeting or similar lightweight fabric (see To cut out, below)
Matching sewing thread

To cut out

1 Measure an existing pillowcase that fits your pillows.
2 For the main pillowcase you will need two rectangles of fabric, the finished size plus seam allowances all round.
3 For the frill, you will need a rectangle of fabric two to three times the measurement right round the end of the pillowcase x the width of the frill plus seam allowances (the frill in the picture is 10cm (4in) wide). This piece can be joined if necessary to save fabric.
4 Pieces as simple as this can be marked out straight on to the wrong side of the fabric with tailor's chalk and cut out.

To make up

1 Join the frill into a ring and neaten one long edge twice (see page 71). Fold the frill in half widthways and then in half again, and make a large hand stitch at each fold on the unstitched edge. Use these stitches as guides when sewing the frill to the pillowcase.
2 Make three rows of gathering stitches along the unstitched edge (see page 70), starting from the seam. Pull up to fit the open end of the pillowcase.
3 With right sides together, lay the two rectangles for the pillowcase one on the other, then pin and stitch the sides and one end. Fold the open end in half (seams together) and mark both folds with a hand stitch to correspond with those on the frill.
4 With right sides together, lay the frill on the open end of the pillowcase, matching the seam on the frill to one of the seams on the pillowcase and the corresponding marker stitches to each other or to the second seam. With the frill underneath, pin all round, adjusting the gathers to fit. Stitch with the pillowcase on top and neaten the edges with zigzag. Remove the third row of gathering. Press the seam to lie inside the pillowcase.

frilled curtain

This frilled muslin curtain makes a change from the ubiquitous nylon net. Leave it free to move gently in the breeze, or tie it back with a fancy ribbon tie as shown in the photograph. It will look soft and pretty either way. Hang the curtain from rings on a pole.

Use ordinary cotton muslin to make up the curtain. If this is not available, cotton voile or organdie would be viable alternatives – they will give a similar effect but might be too formal for a country cottage, although ideal for more sophisticated or modern interiors.

You will need
Cotton muslin (see To cut out, below)
Narrow curtain tape
Matching sewing thread
Curtain hooks

To cut out
1 The main piece will measure the width of the window plus extra for

gathering up plus 5cm (2in) each side for neatening x the length of the window plus 5cm (2in) for the hem and 30cm (12in) for the frill.
2 When cutting muslin, it is important to cut on the grain so that it will hang properly. To do this, either pull out a thread right across the width close to one end or, using very sharp scissors, cut across the width close to the end, following a thread. Measure from this straight edge and cut out. Voile or organdie may be finished in a way that makes it impossible to do this; in this case, cut across one end at right angles to the selvedge (use the corner of a table as a guide).

To make up
1 Neaten curtain sides and press 5cm (2in) to the wrong side, following the line of a thread. Press, pin and stitch.
2 At the top, press 1cm (⅜in) on to the wrong side. Then press 15cm (6in) on to the wrong side, taking great care to make the fold exactly along a thread; the neatened edge should then also lie along the line of a thread. Pin and stitch close to the edge.
3 Lay the curtain tape on the stitched edge of the frill on the wrong side and pin in place along both sides, turning the ends under at the inner edge of the curtain sides. Stitch both sides close to the edge of the tape. Pull up the strings on the tape so that the curtain fits the window and knot off.
4 Turn up the hem on the lower edge along a thread, turn under the raw edge, press, and stitch close to the inner folded edge.
5 Put hooks into the tape, spacing them evenly along the length.

fancy bag

Most people could find a use for this charming little bag – make one as a gift and you will probably be besieged by requests for more. The one in the photograph is made from two layers of silk taffeta, giving a luxurious appearance although, as it uses very little fabric, it is comparatively cheap to make.

The bag can, however, be made from almost any fabric, although if the outer layer is made from wool or heavier fabrics it would be a good idea to use a traditional lining for the inner layer so that it does not look too heavy.

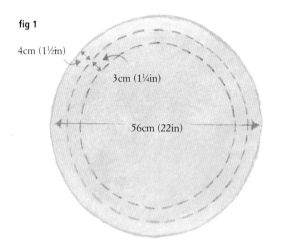

fig 1

4cm (1½in)

3cm (1¼in)

56cm (22in)

You will need

Fabric for outer layer and lining (see To cut out, below)
Contrasting fabric for rosette and to cover button (see To cut out, below)
Button to cover
Fancy cord, 70cm (28in) long
Matching sewing thread

To cut out

1 You will need enough fabric to cut out two circles each 56cm (22in) in diameter, one for the outer layer and one for the lining, and enough contrasting fabric to cut a circle 20cm (8in) in diameter for the rosette, plus a scrap to cover the button.
2 Cut out the three circles and a tiny one the right size to cover the button.

To make up

1 With right sides together, lay the two circles for the bag one on the other and pin. Stitch round the edge with a small seam allowance, leaving a small gap through which to turn out the bag.
2 Turn the bag right side out and slipstitch the gap neatly. Press the seam, making sure it does not roll over to either side.
3 Mark two circles on the lining, 4cm (1½in) and 7cm (2¾in) from the circumference. Stitch round on the lines, forming a channel (fig 1).
4 On the right side only, cut between the two lines of stitching and neaten with buttonhole stitch (see page 50).
5 Thread the cord into the channel through the cut and pull up.
6 Make the rosette (see page 71). Make two rows of tiny gathering stitches all round the edge of the 20cm (8in) circle of fabric. Draw up tightly, forming the centre of the rosette, and knot firmly. Cover the button (see page 52) and sew on to the centre, hiding the stitches. Pull out the folded edge to form a wavy circle. Stitch in place on the bag.

pintucked curtains

Pintucks add texture – all that is needed to decorate these small curtains for the doors of a beautiful cupboard. Lightweight and closely woven fabric is the easiest to pintuck and will also be dustproof; avoid slippery or shiny fabrics, as they might be difficult to control for this technique.

You will need

Lightweight, closely woven fabric (see To cut out, below)
Matching sewing thread

To cut out

1 Stitch a few pintucks on a measured piece of your chosen fabric, measure again and use these figures to work out how many pintucks to make and how much extra fabric to allow for them.
2 Decide on the finished size of the curtains, making them long enough for the top and bottom edges to be hidden behind the door. Add to the width the extra amount required for the pintucks, plus turnings on each side, and cut out.
3 Cut out four bands of fabric, each the same width as the finished curtains plus seam allowances x 10cm (4in) deep

approximately (depending on the finished size of the curtains), to use as binding at the tops and bottoms.

To make up

1 Make a series of pintucks lengthways right across each curtain, or according to your design (see page 72).

2 Neaten the sides by folding the edges over twice on to the wrong side, then pin and stitch in place. Press lightly.

3 Fold and press the bindings in half lengthways. Press the seam allowances on the sides and ends on to the wrong side. Lap the bindings closely round the top and bottom of each curtain, then pin and topstitch on the edges of the binding. If the curtains will hang from wires, stitch a second row across each end to form channels.

chevrons & scallops

Chevrons are triangles made from striped fabric formed into V shapes. For an exotic look, use processions of chevrons around the edges of bedspreads, curtains or tablecloths or decorate the Garden Pavilion (see page 42) with them. Similar shapes, minus the stripes, can also be used as decoration although, strictly speaking, they are not chevrons.

Scallops are a series of curves cut along an edge as decoration. They can be tiny and hand finished to make pretty edgings for bedlinen, or large and finished with facings to decorate cushions or anything else appropriate which needs trimming.

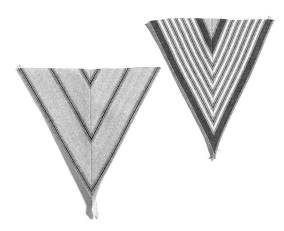

Making chevrons

1 Cut out a right-angled triangle from paper, lay this on some striped fabric and mark round it (see page 108 for two patterns). Turn the pattern over, lay it on the fabric in the same position on the stripes as before and mark round it again (fig 1). Cut out both triangles, lay the pattern on them again to make sure they are absolutely accurate and trim if necessary.

2 With right sides together, lay the triangles one on the other, then pin and stitch the long bias-cut edges together (fig 2). Open out and press the seam open (fig 3). The stripes must match exactly, so take great care to pin the triangles together accurately. To achieve perfect results, practice first.

3 Make several chevrons cut from the same position on the stripes, so that they are all the same when joined. Neaten the edges (see opposite). The chevrons can then be sewn on to a band or tape one by one (fig 4). Because of the striped pattern, chevrons must be made separately, but unstriped triangles can be cut as a row and used in the same way as striped ones.

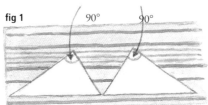

fig 1   90°   90°

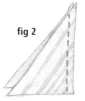

fig 2

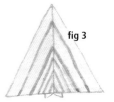

fig 3

band folded over top of chevrons and topstitched

fig 4   bias seams

Making scallops

- Rows of scallops are usually cut in one long piece (fig 5). Use the diagrams on pages 106–107 for patterns.
- For larger scallops, fold up a strip of paper of the required length in concertina style, draw a scallop shape on the top and cut through all the layers. Cut out in fabric.

fig 5

Finishes

Making facings

1 Using the piece to be faced as a pattern, cut a facing from matching or contrasting fabric. Trim off about 3mm (⅛in) around each curve or point to help the facing roll on to the wrong side.

2 Lay the two pieces right sides together. Pin the edges together, and stitch around the curved or pointed sides. Trim and clip the seam allowance using very sharp scissors. It is unnecessary to staystitch the points, unless the fabric is prone to fraying or will receive a lot of wear, perhaps on a cushion or pillowcase.

3 Turn right side out and press.

Other finishes

Whether scallops or chevrons need to be faced depends on how they will be used. If the wrong side will not be seen, finish in either of the following ways:

● Use braid, fringe, binding or piping (see pages 80–83), set on in the appropriate way.

● Turn the edges on to the wrong side, press, then topstitch or hem.

Using chevrons and scallops

● Individual chevrons and scallops can be set into seams or edges singly or stitched on to tape, ribbon or a band and used to make items such as tie-backs or pelmets.

● Chevrons often look best when overlapped slightly and with a small tuck made in the middle, although they can also be used flat. This varies with the particular stripe.

● Individual scallops usually look nicest laid edge to edge so that each complete curve can be seen.

● Make loops on the top of a row of scallops or chevrons to thread on to a curtain pole.

● Small scallops are traditionally finished with buttonhole stitch. Using one of the patterns on pages 106–107, cut out a row along the edge of a strip of fabric which will not fray easily. Buttonhole stitch the edge and use to make edgings and frills on tablecloths or sheets.

● A quicker method, which looks just as pretty, is to finish the edge with a close zigzag stitch instead of hand stitches.

bindings

A binding is a folded strip which is wrapped around a cut edge to finish it. It can be either ready-made (available from haberdashery shops) or made from strips of cut and folded fabric. To take full advantage of its decorative potential, it is usual to use a binding in a contrasting colour and/or texture to the rest of the article.

Ready-made bindings

Two distinct types of ready-made binding are available, and it is important to distinguish between them. Both types are made in a range of weights, so choose one to suit the weight of the fabric used for the rest of the item. Cards of 'bias binding' are intended for binding seams and hems only, and usually fade and fray rapidly.

- Bias woven bindings – these are pliable, so can be used around both straight and curved edges.

- Straight woven bindings – these are not pliable, so cannot be used on curves, but can be mitred for corners.

Fabric bindings

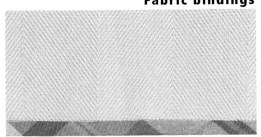

These can be cut either on the bias or straight, and from different weights and types of fabric. The width for bias and straight-cut bindings is worked out in the same way: double the finished width, plus the width of two seam allowances.

Making fabric bindings

1 Mark the strips straight on to the fabric, either on the bias (see page 21) or on the straight grain. Cut out.
2 Working on the ironing board, fold and press the strips in half, with the right side on the outside. Fold and press both the seam allowances on to the wrong side. Take care not to stretch bias-cut bindings.

Setting on bindings

NB The edge to be bound does not require a seam allowance.

fig 1

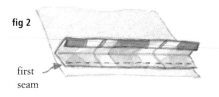
fig 2

first seam

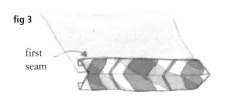
fig 3

first seam

Fabric binding, both types

1 Open out the binding and lay the right side of one edge on the wrong side of the piece to be bound, so that when it is stitched and folded into position the binding will wrap closely around the cut edge. Pin into position (fig 1).
2 Stitch along the crease marking the seam allowance (fig 2).
3 Press the binding to lie over the edge and then back through the central crease on to the right side (fig 3).
4 Pin the free edge of the binding in place along the stitching line on the right side (fig 4). Machine stitch close to the edge of the binding.

Ready-made binding, both types

- Lap the binding around the cut edge, then pin and stitch from the right side through both edges of the binding.
  This is the quickest method and works with some bindings, but on others the stitching misses the underneath edge. Because of this, it is often quicker to use method below.
- Open out the binding and lap one side, with the right side up, over the wrong side of the cut edge, then pin and stitch. Fold the binding so that the second side lies on the right side of the fabric, then pin and stitch close to the edge of the binding.

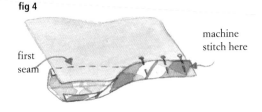
fig 4

first seam

machine stitch here

decorative edgings

There are an enormous variety of edgings, braids and fringes from which to choose, and they can be used to decorate the edges of loose covers, cushions, curtains and tablecloths – in fact, almost anything you make.

An attractive edging will add a finishing flourish to an otherwise plain project. The edging chosen should not be too heavy for the fabric and can either match or contrast with it in both colour and texture. It is important to check that the braid or edging is pliable if it is to be used to trim around curved edges or corners.

Edgings

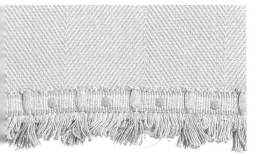

Edgings always have one decorative edge and one plain edge. The latter is used for stitching the edging to the fabric; it is not meant to be seen and should be hidden in a seam or under an edge.

● Broderie Anglaise edgings are made from embroidered fabric and can be sewn in the same way as the fabric forming the rest of the item, set into edges or seams either flat or gathered, or tucked to form frills.

● Frilled, fringed or pleated edgings are usually made with a band or tape on the opposite side to set them in with. The band or tape can be set into a seam or tucked under an edge and topstitched in place.

Braids

Braids are two-sided and are usually used close to the finished edge. They must be sewn down along both edges either by hand or by machine, whichever is appropriate.

● Some braids will be flattened by machining over them, and these should be sewn on by hand. With others this is not a problem and the machine stitches sink into the texture of the braid, rendering them almost invisible.

● On some braids machine stitches will stand out too much, necessitating hand sewing. If avoiding miles of hand sewing is an important factor, experiment with sample lengths before buying large amounts of braid.

Fringes

Although there are plenty of ready-made fringes available, it is more creative and much more fun to make your own.

Making fringes
This is simplicity itself: pull threads away from a straight-cut edge and, hey presto, you have a fringe! Sometimes a needle will help if the threads are difficult to remove; it is usually easier to pull away only one or two threads at a time. Experiment with scraps, fringing them in both directions to test the different effects. Try cutting the edge with pinking shears.

● Cut strips, fringe them and set them into seams. Of course, common sense must prevail: it would be useless setting these fringes into something that requires frequent washing, but on decorative items which are not handled much home-made fringes have a quality which is hard to beat.

● To make a firmer fringe, cut a strip along the selvedge, fringe out the cut side and set the selvedge into the seam.

● Use zigzag stitch to prevent fringes fraying further.

● Some fabrics fray easily, and make lush fringes with little effort; look for these in your remnant bag.

● Silky fabrics make the most striking fringes because they are so bright, but some cotton fabrics are just as successful where more subtle fringing effects are required.

piping

Piping probably originated as a method of strengthening seams: saddles and suitcases still testify to this. Nowadays, piping is used merely as decoration, but it is hard to imagine some things made without it – loose covers without piping look quite bald, and cushion covers somewhat skimped. Luckily, this is one of the easiest and quickest techniques to master – so get piping!

Choosing piping

Piping is either made from piping cord, which is then covered with strips of bias-cut fabric, or is manufactured as a finished decorative cord with an integral tape with which to set it in. Both types of cord are available from haberdashery shops, but it is rare to come across ready-made piping in a good selection of colours and it is often very expensive, so it is usually best to make it yourself. If the finished article will be washed, check that the piping cord is pre-shrunk. It is also a good idea to wash the main fabric and that used for the piping, in case they have different rates of shrinkage.

Piping cord

● Piping cord is made in a range of thicknesses and is available by the metre (yard). It is usually made from cotton.
● Choose the piping cord before the covering fabric and wrap a corner of the fabric around it to see how the finished piping will look and feel.

Ready-made piping

● Ready-made piping is available in many types, some soft and glossy, some stiffer and with a matt finish.
● When choosing piping, check that the tape edge is pliable enough to use round curves if this will be necessary, as some are rather stiff .

Fabric for piping

● Home-made piping has the great advantage that it can be made from many types of fabric, and thus in a wider range of colours.
● Contrasting textures can also be used: for example, satin on velvet or wool, shiny glazed cottons on matt cotton.
● Another decorative option is to use patterned fabrics to cover the cord. Because the fabric is bias cut, stripes look particularly good and go well with checks, plains or other patterns. Alternatively, use plain piping on patterned, striped or checked fabrics.
● Closely woven fabric makes the best piping. It should relate in weight to the fabric used to make the rest of the item and not be over stiff or soft.
● Avoid using fabric with a noticeably different warp and weft, as it may twist when cut on the bias.

Making piping

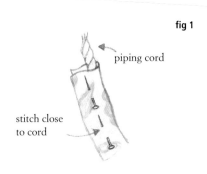

fig 1

piping cord

stitch close to cord

Preparing the bias strips

1 To work out how wide to cut the bias strips, fold a corner of the fabric on the bias around the piping cord, put in a pin close to the cord and allow for seam allowance on both sides. Measure and mark out enough bias strips (see page 21) for all the piping needed for the job.
2 Cut the cord into pieces of the required length. Roll small pieces of sticky tape around the ends to prevent them unravelling.
3 Join the fabric strips (see page 21) into lengths to match the pieces of cord.

Making up the piping

A zip (one-sided) foot should be used whenever machining piping and setting it into seams. This enables the stitches to be made right up against the piping so that the result is well defined.

As there will be three rows of stitching on the finished seam, use larger stitches for the first two rows to avoid stiffening it.
1 Fold a length of joined bias strips in half around the cord, with the right side outside. Use a pin to hold it at the beginning (fig 1).

2 Stitch close to the cord. Do not use pins after the start: it is easier to wrap a short length of fabric around the cord, stitch, wrap another length and carry on in this way to the end. The fabric should be folded snugly around the cord but not stretched.

● Avoid pulling the top layer of fabric over the under layer, as this will cause the bias strip to twist.

● Avoid stitching on to the piping cord – the cover should be able to move along the cord and the stitching line should not be visible in the final seam.

Setting piping into a seam

The method is exactly the same for both ready-made and home-made piping. It is usually quicker and easier to pin but not tack when using piping. If this makes you nervous, do tack – but please experiment first using pins only!

1 Lay the made-up piping on the right side of one of the pieces to be seamed, with the cut edges next to that of the seam, and pin the end (fig 2). Stitch close to the edge of the seam, keeping everything flat and tensioning the fabric if necessary (see page 27).

2 Lay the second side of the seam on the first, right sides together, over the piping. Pin and stitch tight against the cord, using the normal stitch size and tensioning the fabric if necessary.

3 Press the seam allowance to one side; the piping will automatically lie to the other. Avoid pressing over the piping.

Curves and corners

1 Pin the piping on to the side on which it will eventually lie and stitch close to

the piping. Put on the second side of the seam as before.

2 Press the seam allowances to one side, clipping to allow them to lie flat or, if too full, pressing into small triangular tucks (figs 3 and 4).

● When piping tightly curved seams, it may be necessary to clip through the seam allowance (or tape) of the piping in order to make it lie flat before pinning on the second side of the seam.

● When piping will lie on the outside of a corner, you will need to clip into the corner at the pinning stage (fig 5). Pin up to the corner, clip through the tape or seam allowance to the stitching line at the corner, bend the piping round the corner and continue pinning. Or, on an inside corner, form a fold (fig 5).

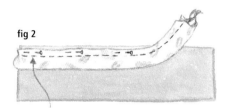

fig 2

first row of stitching

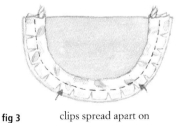

fig 3   clips spread apart on outward curve

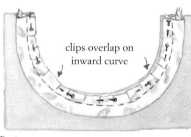

clips overlap on inward curve

fig 4

piping on outside corner

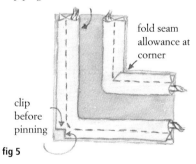

fold seam allowance at corner

clip before pinning

fig 5

Setting piping into an edge

1 Set in the piping in the same way as before to the pressing stage.

2 Fold the facing back or turn right side out in the usual way. Press and edge

stitch if required, using the zip foot.

3 Clip the seam allowance and press from the wrong side. Avoid pressing over the piping so as not to flatten it.

piped & frilled cushion

Making new cushions is one of the easiest ways of revitalizing a tired colour scheme or adding a new look to an old sofa. Choose three or four complementary fabrics and use the remnants from one cushion to trim another with piping, frills or a combination of both. Setting a frill into a cushion cover is very simple: just take care to pin the loose edges of the frill to the cushion cover so that they do not get caught up in the seam.

fig 1

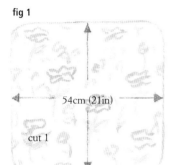

cut 1

54cm (21in)

fig 2

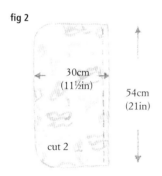

30cm (11½in)

54cm (21in)

cut 2

You will need

Fabric (see To cut out, below)
Thin wadding, 54cm (21in) square
2m (2¼yd) piping cord
Matching sewing thread
40cm (16in) zip
50cm (20in) square cushion pad

To cut out

1 Cut out one piece of fabric 54cm (21in) square for the top of the cushion. Round off the corners (fig 1).
2 Cut out two pieces of fabric, each 30 x 54cm (11½ x 21in), for the back of the cushion. Round off two corners on each piece (fig 2).
3 Across the width of the fabric, cut out enough strips 11cm (4in) wide to make a frill 4m (4¼yd) long when joined. Cut out enough bias strips to make piping (see pages 82–83).

To make up

1 Join the frill into a ring. Turn 5mm (¼in) on one edge on to the wrong side and stitch along the fold. Trim the cut edge, turn over the same amount again and stitch over the first row of stitches. Press. Make three rows of gathering stitches on the other edge (see page 70). Fold the frill in half widthways and then in half again, make a large hand stitch at each fold on the edge with gathering stitches. Unfold the frill and pull up the gathering stitches to fit the cushion and anchor on a pin.
2 Join the piping cord into a ring by unravelling a little at each end, then overlapping and twisting the strands together neatly, wrapping a thread around them and stitching through a few times to hold the join securely. Make the cord marginally shorter than the edges of the cushion, as it will stretch slightly when it is stitched on.

3 Join the bias strips into a ring marginally shorter than the piping cord. Wrap the strip round the cord, stretching it slightly, and stitch (see pages 82–83).
4 With right sides together, lay the two back pieces one on the other. Lay the zip centrally on the centre seam and put pins into the seam, to indicate the opening. Stitch from the pin to the edge at each end with a 3cm (1in) seam allowance, backstitch at both ends and neaten the edges. Press the seam open and set in the zip (see page 48).
5 Lay the square for the top of the cushion on the wadding, right side up, then pin and stitch all round.
6 Lay the piping on the right side of the square, cut edges together, and pin, stretching the cord slightly. Machine stitch all round near the edge, using a large stitch and zip foot.
7 With right sides together, lay the frill on the square over the piping, matching raw edges and a hand stitch to each of the corners. Pin, evening out the gathers all round – this will take a long time! Make the gathers extra full at the corners to prevent the frills looking skimped. When everything is exactly right, knot the gathering threads. Stitch all round close to the edge, using a large stitch and zip foot.
8 With right sides together, lay the back, with zip open, on the top square, over the frill and piping. Pin the layers together and stitch all round close to the piping, using a zip foot.
9 Turn the cover right side out and remove the third row of gathering. Press the seam and frill. Use the point of the iron to press into the gathers, do not flatten them with the iron.
10 Insert the cushion pad through the opening and close the zip.

throw

This pretty throw can be used in a boat or draped over a sofa or bed. The top layer can be made from many types of fabric – cotton, linen, silk or wool – depending on where it will be used. A piece of patchwork would look pretty framed in this way. Cut the pieces neat and true, with accurately mitred corners, and success will be ensured. This is another project that can be completed in an evening.

fig 1

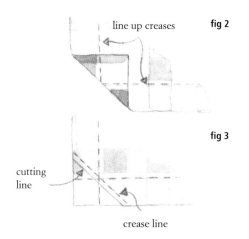

line up creases   fig 2

fig 3

cutting line

crease line

You will need

Enough fabric for:
  top layer, inner layer and backing
  (see Fabric and To cut out, below)
Matching sewing thread

Fabric

The throw is composed of three layers, each made from different fabric:

● Top layer of lightweight fabric. Printed cotton chintz was used for the throw in the photograph.

● Inner layer to give bulk to the throw. A blanket, soft woollen fabric, terylene wadding or towelling would all be suitable.

● Backing of strong hardwearing fabric, with a design that complements that of the top layer. Checked moiré was used for this one.

To cut out

1 Decide on the size of the throw. Cut out pieces to exactly this size from the fabrics for the top and inner layers. Join widths if the fabric is not wide enough. There is no need to neaten raw edges. Use a large set square or the corner of a table to ensure that the sides are at right angles to each other.

2 Cut out the backing 24cm (10in) larger both ways than the other two pieces; this allows for 12cm (5in) hems on each side. Use a set square as before to keep the piece square.

3 To mitre the corners on the backing, fold and press the hems on each side over on to the right side accurately and firmly, and open out (fig 1). Fold up a corner, lining up the creases as shown in fig 2, and press. Open out again and draw a line 2cm (¾in) from the diagonal crease (fig 3). Cut along this line. Mitre all four corners in the same way.

To make up

1 Press the backing until it is completely flat, then press 2cm (¾in) accurately on to the wrong side on all four sides. With right sides together, fold each mitred corner in half, bringing the neatened edges together, and pin (fig 4). Stitch with a 2cm (¾in) seam allowance from the fold to the creases at the outer edge, backstitching at each end. Press the four mitred seams open, re-press the hems and lay the backing out flat with the hems on top.

2 Press the top and inner layers so that they are completely flat. Lay the top layer right side up on the wadding, pin all round and stitch close to the edge using a large stitch.

3 Lay this double layer on the backing, right side up, tucking the sides under the mitred corners and hems. Smooth out flat and pin all round the inner edge of the hem, through all layers (fig 5). Check that the underside of the throw is completely smooth before stitching. Topstitch close to the edge; avoid using a stitch smaller than necessary, as this will stiffen the seam and encourage stretching.

fig 4

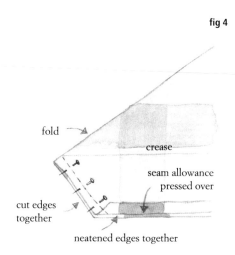

fold

crease

seam allowance pressed over

cut edges together

neatened edges together

fig 5

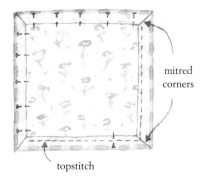

mitred corners

topstitch

bound curtains with bows

This pair of unlined curtains would add a light and airy touch to any room. They are made with contrasting bindings on the inside edge and hem, and are tied to a pole with bows. Make them from a medium-weight unbleached cotton with chequered binding, as in the photograph, or go for glamour and use raw silk with a contrasting silk binding – or any other combination that takes your fancy.

You will need
Main fabric (see To cut out, below)
Contrasting fabric, for binding (see To cut out, below)
Matching sewing thread

To cut out
1 Work out the finished size of the curtains, and add a 5cm (2in) seam allowance to the outer edge and top only. Cut out.

2 Decide on the number of ties required, a pair every 25cm (10in) is a rough guide. Work out the length and width of ties: a finished size of 70 x 8cm (28 x 3in) would suit a large window. Double the width and add a seam allowance all round each tie.

3 The binding on the curtains shown in the photograph is cut on the straight of the fabric (either cut all the strips across the grain or all parallel to the selvedge) and is 8cm (3in) wide. Cut out the binding to twice this width plus two seam allowances, and as long as the length plus width of the curtains plus two seam allowances. Join the fabric if necessary to make it long enough, and add a little to allow for mitres at the corners. The fabric for the binding should not be thicker than that used for the curtains.

To make up
1 Press each tie in half lengthways, right

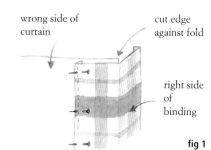

wrong side of curtain

cut edge against fold

right side of binding

fig 1

sides out, press the seam allowances on to the wrong side. Topstitch close to the edge and across the ends.

2 Join the binding with flat seams to make two pieces, each one long enough for one curtain. Press the seams open. Press the bindings in half lengthways, right sides out, and press the seam allowances onto the wrong side. Be very careful not to stretch the edges, as this will stop the binding lying flat when it is stitched.

3 Starting at the top, lap the binding round the inside edge of one of the curtains, so that the fold is against the cut edge. Pin one edge of the binding to the curtain on the wrong side only (fig 1). At the lower end, fold and press the binding neatly to form a mitre to fit round the corner. Trim away some of the surplus from underneath. Continue to pin along the hem to the outer edge of the curtain. Stitch close to the edge of the binding; do not stretch the fabric, although it may help to keep it all smooth if the fabric is tensioned slightly as it is stitched (see page 27).

4 Fold the second side of the binding in place to lie on the right side of the curtain. Pin the edge as before, folding and pressing the mitre at the corner. Stitch close to the edge as before.

5 Fold over the outer edge of the curtain and press the seam allowance over on to the wrong side. Pin and stitch close to the edge from top to bottom.

6 Neaten the top edge of the curtain and press over on to the wrong side. Pin and stitch close to the edge.

7 Space pairs of ties evenly across the top edge and pin the ends to the stitching line on the wrong side of the curtain. Machine stitch across the ends, forming a cross in a square (fig 2).

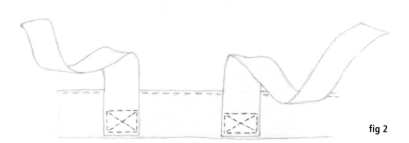

fig 2

squab cushion

This squab cushion presents an opportunity to practise scalloping, piping and sewing neat points, and will transform a plain wooden chair into one which is both pretty and comfortable. Make one for a bedroom chair or a set for the dining room.

You will need

Furnishing or dressmaking fabric, strong enough to withstand being sat on (see To draw the pattern, below)

Curtain or other lining fabric, in same quantity as main fabric

Wadding, 2 or 3 layers for seat and single thin layer for skirt

Matching sewing thread

Piping cord, to length of skirt (see below)

To draw the pattern

1 Measure the seat of the chair and draw out the shape on paper, adding seam allowances all round (fig 1).

2 Measure from one inner corner on the back edge round the side, front and side to the other inner corner. This is the length for the 'skirt'; draw a line to this length. Draw another line parallel to it and about 10cm (4in) from it; this is the depth for the skirt. Measure from the inner corner to the outer corner at the back of the seat pattern and mark this off at each end. Divide the remaining length into five equal sections and draw a scallop in each one, using the patterns on pages 106–107 as a guide. Add narrow seam allowances round the scallops and sides, and the usual allowance to the straight edge (fig 2).

3 Measure up the two pattern pieces, add some for bias strips and ties (see To cut out) and work out how much fabric will be required.

To cut out

1 Cut one seat piece and one skirt piece in the main fabric and lining; remember to centre and match the design on the main fabric from seat to skirt. Cut one skirt piece from wadding and two or three layers of wadding for the seat, depending on how much of a cushion effect is required.

2 From the main fabric, cut out a bias strip the same length as the skirt for piping (see pages 82–83).

3 Cut out four strips from the main fabric, 25cm (10in) long and 6cm (2½in) wide, for the ties.

To make up

1 Press each tie in half lengthways, with the right side outside. Open up, fold long raw edges to centre crease, press and fold with raw edges inside, press one end to inside. Stitch close to the pressed edges.

2 Fold the bias strip round the piping cord and stitch (see pages 82–83).

Skirt

1 Lay the skirt on the wadding, right side up, then pin and stitch all round close to the edge.

2 Lay the lining on the skirt, right sides together, then pin and stitch round the scallops and up the sides. Be very accurate at the points, making a sharp turn on the needle at each one. Staystitch the points and the corners at each end and clip through the seam allowance to the stitches; also trim back the seam allowance close to the stitches at the corners. Trim away the seam allowance on the wadding.

3 Turn right side out and press, rolling the seam to lie on the wrong side. Pin the two layers on the top edge of the skirt together and stitch close to the edge. Lay the piping on the top with

fig 1

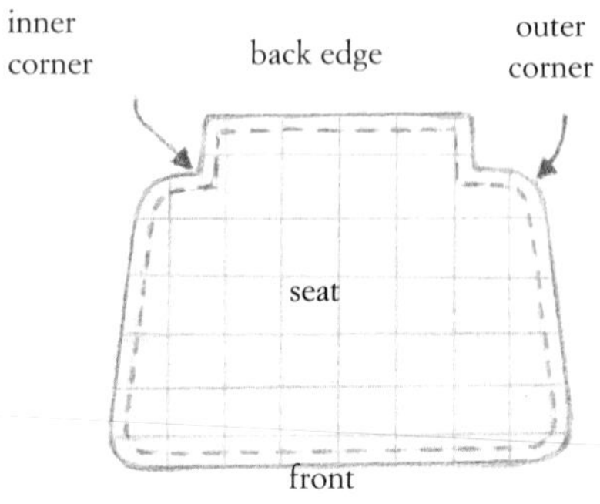

inner corner

outer corner

back edge

seat

front

top edge

side

skirt

10cm (4in)

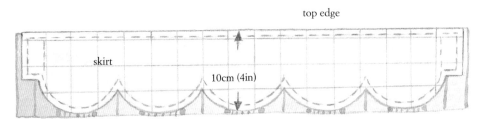

fig 2

fig 3

stitched and pressed

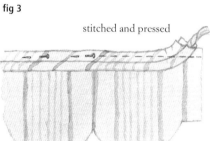

fig 4

stay-
stitch

edges together, twisting it round at each end (fig 3). Stitch close to the piping, and across it at the ends.

Seat

1 Lay the layers of wadding for the seat together. Pin the main fabric on top, right side up, and stitch all round.

2 Lay the seat lining on the seat, right sides together, then pin and stitch the back edges round to the inner corner only. Staystitch all four corners (fig 4). Clip into the two inner corners and trim back to the two back corners. Turn right side out and press, rolling the seam to lie on the wrong side. Pin and stitch the free edges together from one inner corner round to the other.

3 Lay the skirt on the seat, right sides together, matching one end of the skirt to the inner corner on the seat. Pin, and continue pinning all round to the other end of the skirt, which will finish at the other inner corner. Stitch close to the piping, using a zip foot. Turn right side out and press.

4 Fold the cut ends of the ties to the wrong side, pin and machine stitch to the inner corners on the lining.

5 Tie the cushion to the chair.

91

bolster

A plump bolster adds an air of sophistication to a sofa or day bed and makes a deliciously comfortable headrest. Although bolsters look more complicated to make than a square cushion cover, they are in fact surprisingly easy to run up.

You will need

Bolster cushion pad
Plain and checked furnishing fabric (see To cut out, below)
40cm (16in) zip
2 large buttons to cover
Piping cord, twice circumference of bolster
Matching sewing thread

To cut out

1 Mark out a rectangle for the main piece on the wrong side of the checked fabric, measuring the circumference of the bolster x its length, plus 2cm (¾in) seam allowances all round. Cut out. Mark and cut out two bias strips the same length as the circumference, to make piping (see pages 82–83).

2 Mark out two rectangles for the end pieces on the wrong side of the plain fabric, each measuring twice the circumference of the bolster plus 3cm (1¼in) x the radius plus 1.5cm (⅝in).

3 Cut small circles of fabric the right size to cover the buttons (see page 52).

To make up

1 Cut the piping cord in half. Join each piece into a ring by unravelling 3cm (1in) at both ends, overlapping and twisting the strands together neatly. Wrap a thread around them and stitch through a few times to hold the join securely.

2 Join each bias strip into a ring marginally shorter than the piping cord. Wrap the strip around the cord, stretching it slightly, and stitch (see pages 82–83).

3 Fold the main piece in half, right sides and long edges together, lay the zip centrally on the long edge and put pins into the fabric to mark the opening. Stitch from these pins to the end; backstitch at each end. Press open and set in the zip (fig 1); see also page 48.

4 Lay the pieces of piping on the right side, one at each end, cut edges together. Pin and stitch, using a zip foot.

5 Join the end pieces into rings and press the seams open (fig 2). Make three rows of gathering stitches (see page 70) on each side. On each piece, pull up one side to fit the circumference of the bolster, fastening the ends on a pin. Pull the other side up as tight as possible, forming it into a circle, and knot the threads (fig 3).

6 Open the zip. Lay one end of the main piece over the circumference of one end piece, right sides and edges together. Adjust the gathers to fit, even them out and pin. Using a zip foot, stitch from the wrong side of the main piece, close to the piping. Set on the other end piece in the same way. Remove visible gathering threads.

7 Turn right side out, cover the buttons with scraps of the main fabric (see page 52) and stitch on firmly to hold and hide the centres at each end.

8 Put the bolster in the cover and close the zip.

fig 1

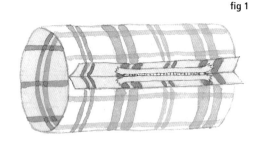

fig 2

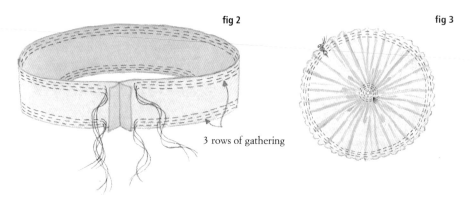

3 rows of gathering

fig 3

chair cover

This chair cover is not difficult to put together, but as the pattern has to be adjusted to fit a specific chair it does involve lots of measuring, and decisions may have to be made about how to adapt it to fit the exact shape of the chair you are covering. It should be well within the capabilities of a confident maker, someone who has already drawn up patterns and completed several successful projects. Do not rush: work slowly and methodically, following the step-by-step instructions and diagrams below and on page 96. Making a toile first using old fabric or cheesecloth would ensure a good fit.

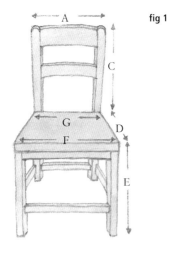

fig 1

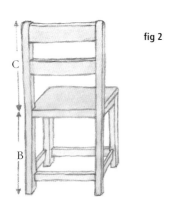

fig 2

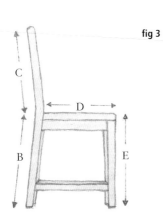

fig 3

You will need

Furnishing fabric (see To draw the
    pattern, below)
Pattern paper
2 buttons to cover
Matching sewing thread

The chair

The chair for this project must be a simple square shape with a straight, plain back, straight legs and a flat seat (figs 1, 2 and 3). Avoid anything with knobs, curves or carving. Plain chairs like this are often available in junk shops, and as some imagination is required to see their potential they should be very cheap!

To measure up

Measure up the chair as shown by the letters A to G in figs 1, 2 and 3. Make the measurement at the top of the back (A) generous, to allow for the thickness of the wood.

To draw the pattern

1 It is probably easiest to trace the pattern diagrams (here and on page 96) and fill in each measurement in the appropriate place, as a preliminary to making the pattern pieces.
2 The pleats at the hem are designed to allow for a slight splay in the legs. Measure round them and check that the lower edge of the skirt will fit round them loosely. If not, work out how much extra width is needed, divide by eight and add one eighth to each of the pleat extensions.
3 If the cover is to trail on the floor, as in the photograph, add 5–8cm (2–3in) to the length of the skirt front, side and

back (before adding the hem allowance).
4 Using the pattern outlines as a guide, draw out each piece to full size, adding the pleat pieces to the skirt and back patterns as indicated. If possible, pin the pattern together to check that all the pieces are correct and will fit the chair or, use old fabric, cheap calico, cheesecloth or sheeting to make up a toile (fabric pattern). Tack it together and fit it on to the chair making any small adjustments necessary.

Back skirt (fig 4)

This has a central inverted pleat (see fig 9 on page 96) and the amount of fabric allowed should be adjusted to suit the pattern on the fabric. To avoid muddling the pattern on the fabric – stripes, for example – fold the fabric into pleats on the lines of the stripes to work out how much to allow for each pleat.

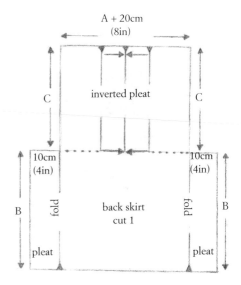

fig 4

fig 5

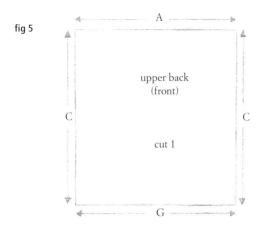

A

upper back
(front)

C   C

cut 1

G

fig 6

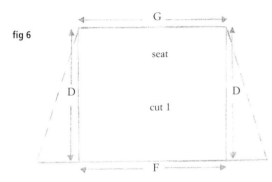

G

seat

D   D

cut 1

F

fig 7

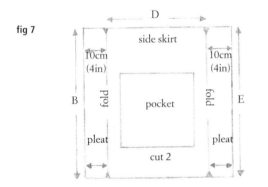

D

side skirt

10cm
(4in)   10cm
                     (4in)

B   fold   pocket   fold   E

pleat   pleat

cut 2

fig 8

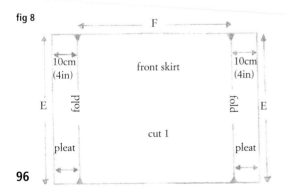

F

10cm
(4in)   front skirt   10cm
                        (4in)

E   fold   fold   E

pleat   pleat

cut 1

96

Seat (fig 6) This may be wider at the front than at the back, and in this case should be cut to the shape indicated by dotted lines on the diagram.

Side and front skirts (figs 7 and 8) Add the same amount as allowed for each back pleat to each side of these pieces.

Pocket (fig 7) Work out the size you want (to take a paper or a book) and draw a square or rectangle.

Finally, add a seam allowance to all edges of all the pattern pieces except the lower edge of the skirt and the top of the pockets, to which you should add hems of 5cm (2in).

Lay out the pattern pieces and work out how much fabric is required.

To cut out

1 Cut out: 1 back skirt, 1 upper back, 1 seat, 1 front skirt, 2 side skirts, 2 pockets, 2 small circles the right size to cover the buttons (see page 52).

2 Mark and clip notches at the top and hem on each side of the side and front skirts, to mark the pleats. Mark and clip notches at the top and hem on the back skirt for the central inverted pleat and the side pleats.

To make up

1 Press the pleats in place down the centre of the back skirt. Pin close to the edge of the pleats from the top, down the centre, to the top of the skirt. Topstitch close to each edge (fig 9).

2 Neaten the hem on the pockets, press on to the wrong side and topstitch. Press the seam allowance on the remaining three sides of each pocket to the wrong side, pin pockets in place on the side skirts and topstitch close to the edge.

NB For the following steps, if the fabric has a tendency to fray, neaten the edges of the seams as they are made. Press all seams open.

3 Lay the side skirts on each side of the back skirt, with right sides together, matching the edges of the pleats B. Pin and stitch.

4 Lay the front skirt on the side skirts with right sides together, matching the edges of the pleats E. Pin and stitch.

5 Neaten the edge of the hem and press to the wrong side. Stitch and press.

6 Fold each pleat through the notches at top and hem, bringing the folds together so that they meet and lie on the seams, forming inverted pleats. Pin at each end to hold in place. Press well using a steam iron to create a sharp crease. Pin or tack the upper edges of the pleats in place to stitch to the seat.

7 Lay the upper back (front) on the upper part of the back skirt, with right sides together. Pin the top A and sides C. Stitch, taking care to leave seam allowances at the lower edges of C free.

8 Lay the seat piece on the upper back, with right sides together, matching at G. Pin and stitch.

9 Pin the sides D and front F to the corresponding edges on the skirt, with right sides together, ensure the pleats are in position and stitch.

10 Cover the two buttons (see page 52) and stitch either side of the pleat in the centre of the back.

11 Drop the cover over the chair.

fig 9

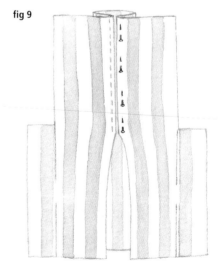

Patterns & motifs

On the following pages you will find the further information that you need for making up some of the projects shown in the earlier chapters. This includes, as relevant, pattern diagrams, cutting layouts and illustrations for the Billowing Curtain, Garden Pavilion, Bean Bag, Rabbit-eared Cushion and the Waistcoat. There are also patterns for scallops and chevrons so that you can choose shapes that will suit projects of your own.

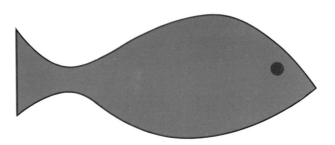

billowing curtain

The instructions on page 32 and the cutting layout (right) and pattern diagram (far right) given here are for making a curtain 2.4m (8ft) long and just under 112cm (44in) wide. If you wish to make a different sized curtain, use the cutting layout as a guide to the pieces that are required (add extra insets for a wider curtain) and work out the measurements to fit your window.

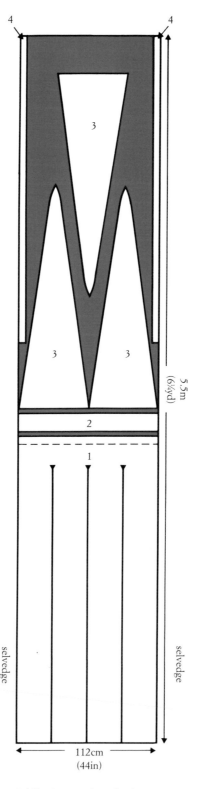

5.5m (6¼yd)

112cm (44in)

selvedge

selvedge

1 billowing curtain main piece
2 billowing curtain heading
3 billowing curtain inset
4 billowing curtain side strip

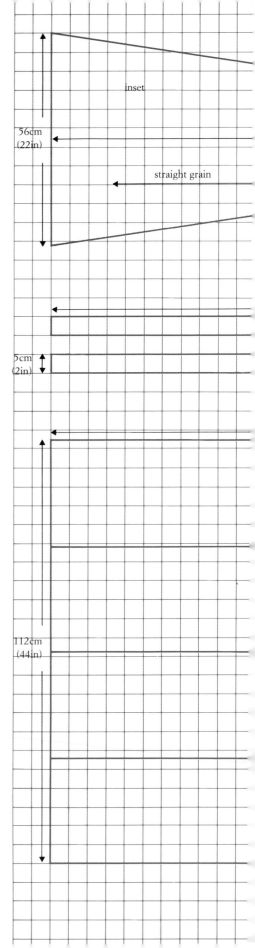

inset

56cm (22in)

straight grain

5cm (2in)

112cm (44in)

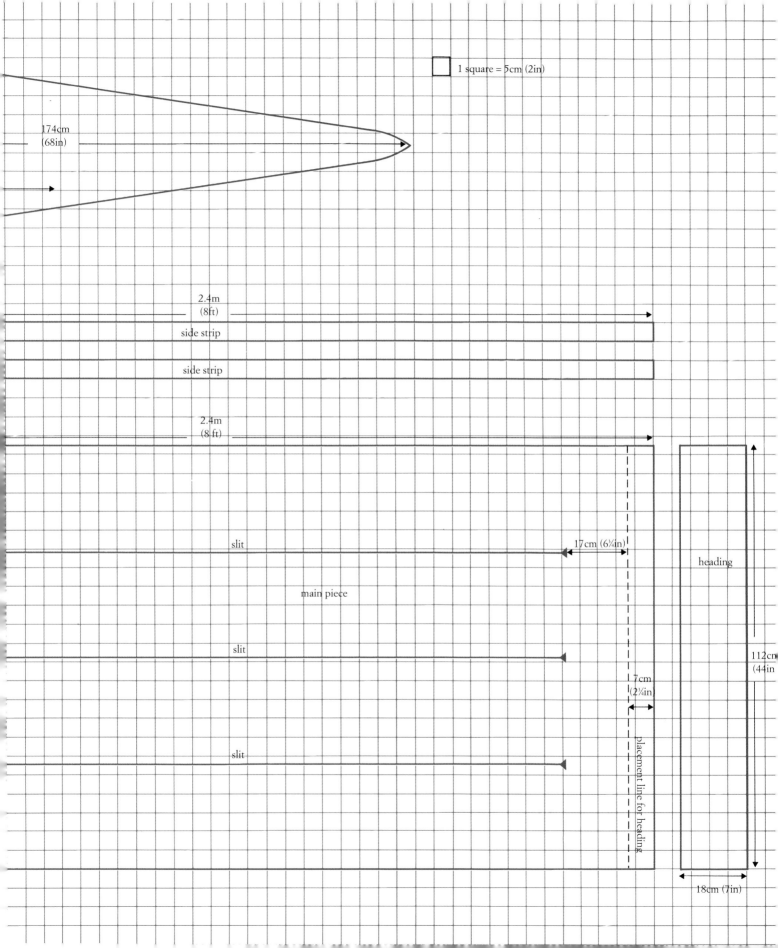

1 square = 5cm (2in)

174cm
(68in)

2.4m
(8ft)

side strip

side strip

2.4m
(8 ft)

slit

17cm (6¼in)

heading

main piece

slit

112cm
(44in)

7cm
(2¼in)

slit

placement line for heading

18cm (7in)

garden pavilion

The pavilion shown in the photograph on pages 42 - 43 is made from a variety of fabrics, the cutting layout (right) is for a pavilion made from one fabric only. If you wish to use more than one fabric, use the cutting layout as a guide to the pieces required and the dimensions given on page 44 to work out how much of each fabric you will need.

The construction diagrams opposite show how to assemble the pavilion frame using the materials and instructions given on page 45.

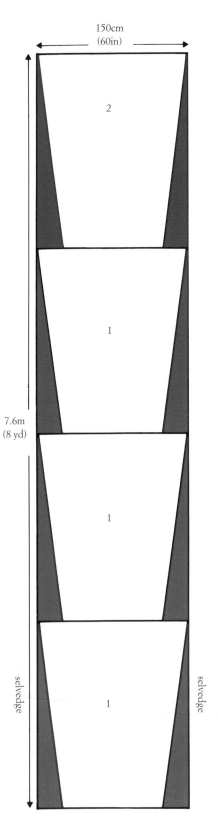

150cm
(60in)

7.6m
(8 yd)

selvedge

selvedge

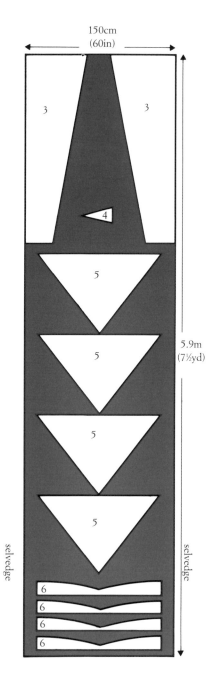

150cm
(60in)

5.9m
(7½yd)

selvedge

selvedge

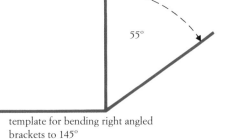

55°

template for bending right angled brackets to 145°

1 pavilion side
2 pavilion door
3 pavilion side front
4 pavilion pennant
5 pavilion roof
6 pavilion valance

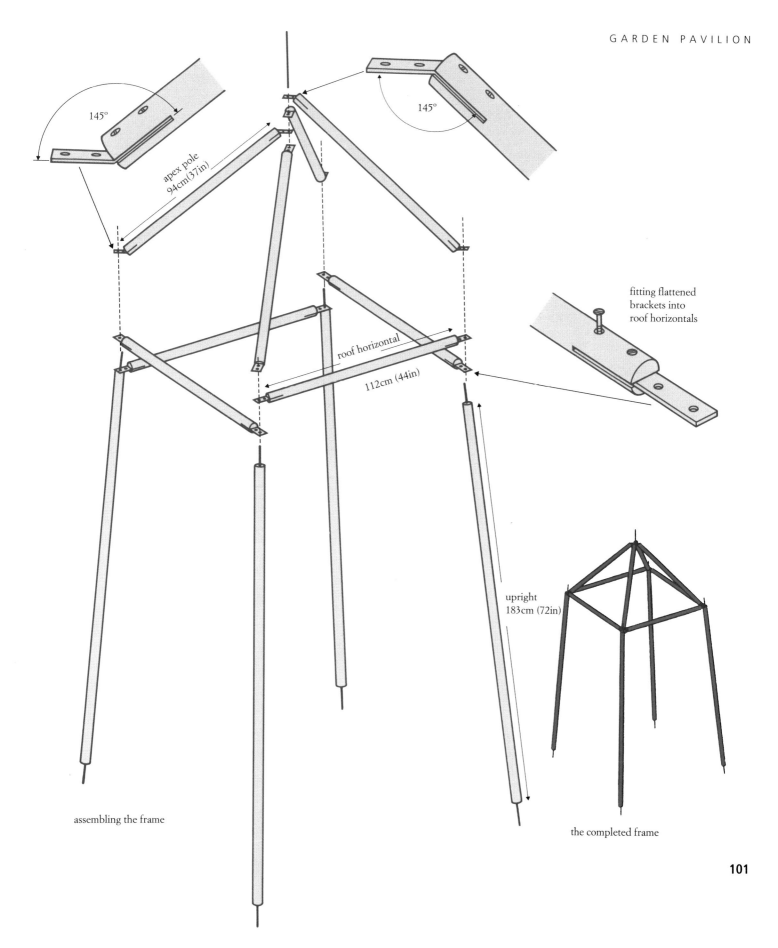

145°

145°

apex pole
94cm(37in)

fitting flattened
brackets into
roof horizontals

roof horizontal

112cm (44in)

upright
183cm (72in)

assembling the frame

the completed frame

waistcoat with Chinese knots

The waistcoat on page 60 is a generous size 12. Slight adjustments to the size can be made at the side seams either by adding extra allowance at the cutting stage (see pattern diagram, right) to make a larger waistcoat, or by taking wider seam allowances at the sides during the making up stage for a smaller one.

cutting layout for main fabric and interfacing

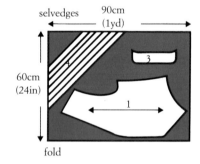

cutting layout for lining fabric

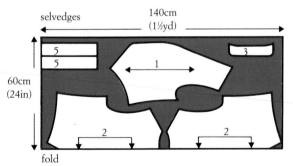

fold

1 waistcoat front
2 waistcoat back
3 waistcoat placket (cut 1)
4 waistcoat bias strips (cut from main fabric only)
5 waistcoat belt

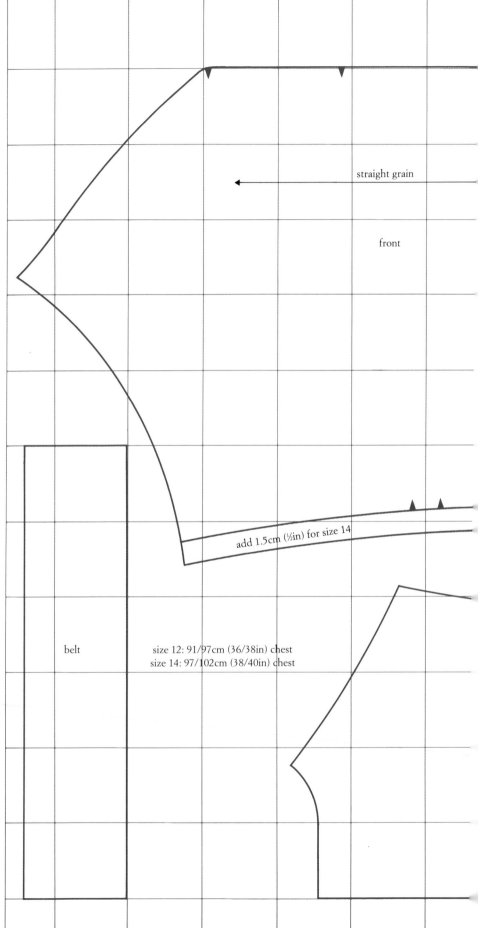

straight grain

front

add 1.5cm (½in) for size 14

belt

size 12: 91/97cm (36/38in) chest
size 14: 97/102cm (38/40in) chest

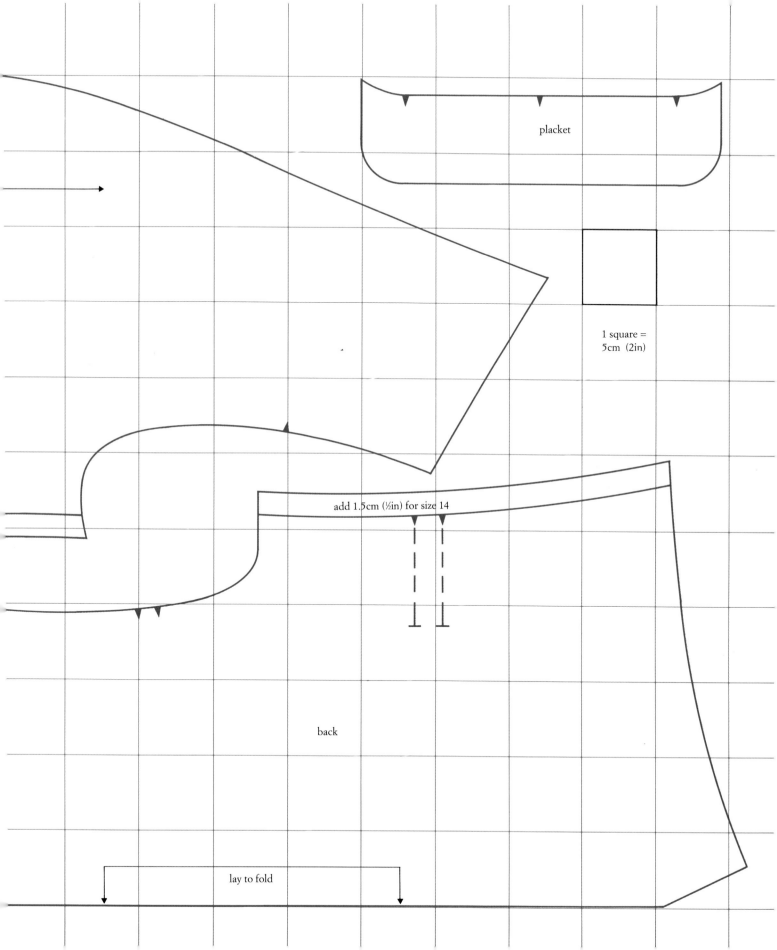

placket

1 square =
5cm (2in)

add 1.5cm (½in) for size 14

back

lay to fold

bean bag

The dimensions on page 64 and the pattern pieces on the pattern diagram (right) are for a large bean bag. If you want to make a small bean bag for a toddler, scale up the pieces using a scale of 1 square = 7.5cm (3in) and refer to the note on safety given on page 64.

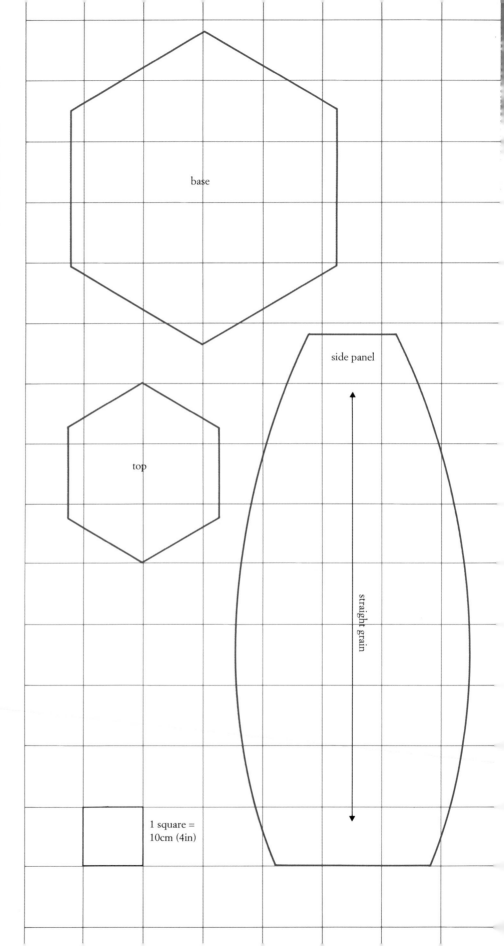

base

top

side panel

straight grain

1 square = 10cm (4in)

rabbit-eared cushion

The pattern diagram (right) shows a quarter of the main piece pattern and half of a tie. Follow the instructions on page 58 to scale up the pattern pieces. Use the cutting layout (below right) to cut all the cushion pieces from the calico or other main fabric. The fish motif (below) is shown full size.

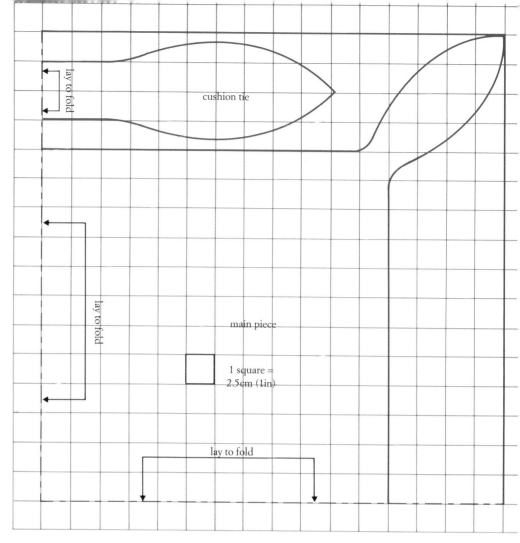

cushion tie

lay to fold

lay to fold

main piece

1 square =
2.5cm (1in)

lay to fold

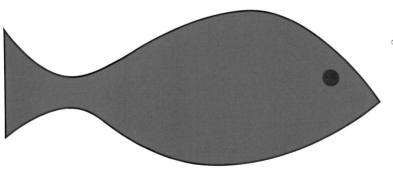

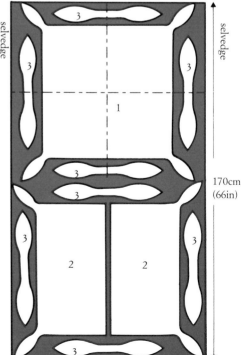

selvedge

selvedge

3

3

3

3

1

3

3

3

3

2

2

3

3

170cm
(66in)

90cm
(36in)

1 rabbit-eared cushion main piece
2 rabbit-eared cushion back piece
3 rabbit-eared tie

scallops

Instructions for making and using scallops are given on pages 78 and 79. Choose whichever scallop design you feel would best enhance your project. All the scallop designs are shown without seam allowances, add a 5mm (¼in) seam allowance along the curved edges and a 1.5cm (⅝in) seam allowance to the straight edge. The wider seam allowance will be easier to stitch into a seam than a narrow one. No scale is given on the grid as the scallops should be enlarged to fit a specific project; choose whichever row of scallops is most appropriate for the design, measure (in centimetres or half inches) one edge along which scallops will be stitched and enlarge or reduce the row of scallops to fit. Rows of scallops should begin and end with a full scallop if possible. They can be cut either along the length of the fabric or across the width.

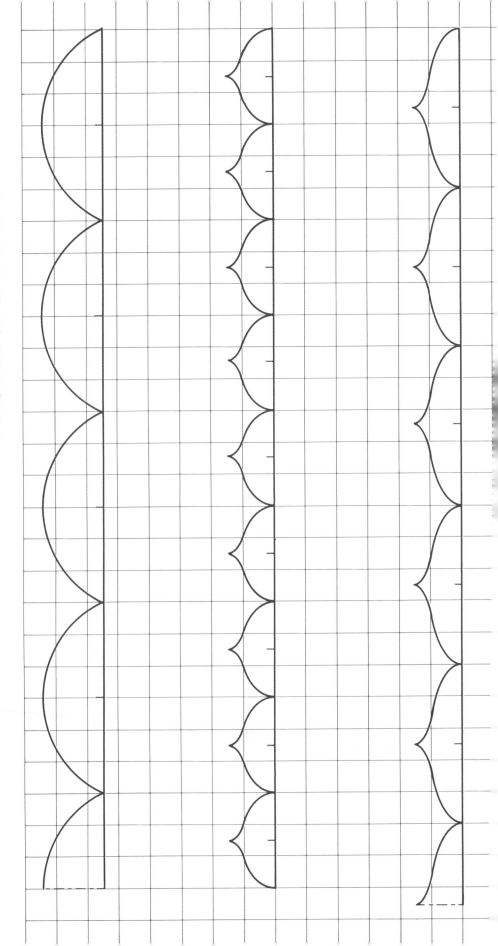

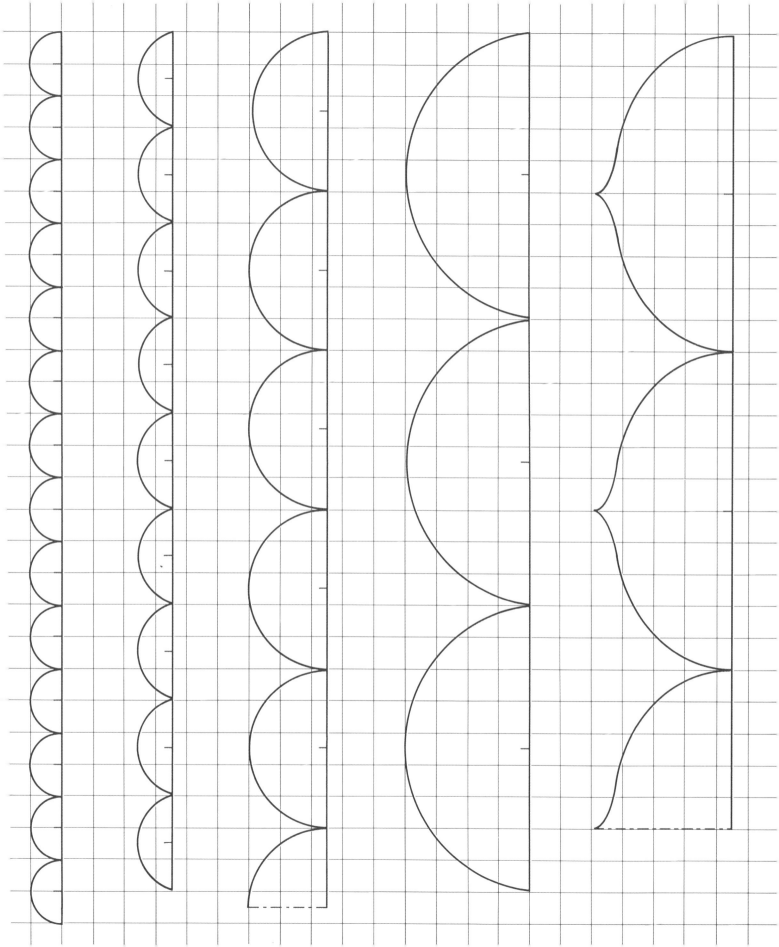

chevrons

Instructions for making and using chevrons are given on pages 78 and 79. True chevrons are each individually made from a pair of striped triangles. Always cut the triangles with the stripes running parallel to the longest edge and join the pairs with the longest bias cut edges together. Different triangles paired together will make differing shapes of chevrons, two long triangles joined will make a pennant shaped chevron while two wider triangles will make a wide chevron more suitable for an edging.

Other edgings with a similar heraldic feel can be created with a combination of squares and triangles and cut as strips (top right). No scale is given on the grid as the chevrons or edgings should be enlarged to fit a specific project; measure (in centimetres or half inches) one edge along which chevrons or edging will be stitched and enlarge the triangles or edgings to fit.

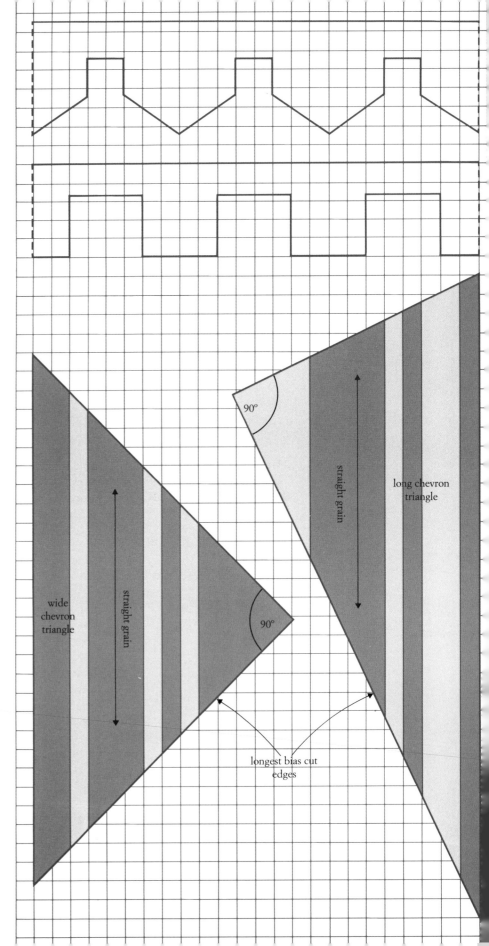

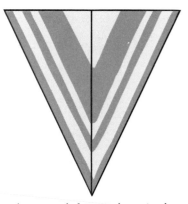

chevron made from two long triangles

chevron made from two wide triangles

index

acknowledgements

The publishers would like to thank the following for their help and for lending fabrics, threads and other items for inclusion in the photography: Elizabeth Baer, Jane Churchill, J & M Davidson, Designer's Guild, Camilla Gavin, John Lewis, Malabar, Ian Mankin, Mulberry, Osborne and Little, Arthur Sanderson and Sons Ltd, F R Street, V V Rouleaux.

Picture credits

Special photography by Martin Brigdale (12–13, 14, 61), Debbie Patterson (2, 3, 63).

Other photography by Jan Baldwin (8, 9, 37, 38, 39, 65, 84 , 87), Chris Drake (67), Frank Herholdt (33, 89, 95), Tom Leighton (15, 40, 41, 74, 75, 77 and 93), Pia Tryde (5, 6, 24, 25, 42, 43, 45, 46, 47, 57, 59, 68, 69, 91), Susan Witney (79).